Coalisland, County Tyrone, in the Industrial Revolution, 1800–1901

Maynooth Studies in Local History

SERIES EDITOR   Raymond Gillespie

This is one of six titles to be published in the Maynooth Studies in Local History series in 2002. The first forty titles were published by Irish Academic Press; the next volumes in the series are being published by Four Courts Press. The publication of this series is a reflection of the continued growth of interest in local and regional history within Ireland in recent years. That interest has manifested itself in diverse ways, including new research about the problems of local and regional societies in the past. These short books seek to make a contribution to that research. As in previous years most are drawn from theses completed as part of the MA in local history at NUI Maynooth.

The new studies published this year are concerned, as their predecessors have been, with the problem of how groups of people within relatively well-defined geographical contexts tried to resolve the problems presented by daily life in the past. Sometimes the areas studied may correspond to administrative units, sometimes not. One local society dealt with this year, Rossin, was an 'unofficial place', known as a distinct community only by those who lived there rather than by administrators. Even such unofficial places had problems in daily life. In some cases those problems had dramatic outcomes. Family jealousies over land and marriage could lead to murder. Elsewhere family networks shaped political actions during the land war. Although local historians are fascinated by the unusual and the violent the daily activities of ordinary life are equally important. The commonplace routines of making a living in an industrial town, worshipping at the local holy well in the way determined by local custom or in the parish church surrounded by one's neighbours are part of the story of the evolution of local societies and all are dealt with in this group of studies.

Taken together these new titles demonstrate yet again, if demonstration is still required, the vibrancy and diversity of the local societies which make up Ireland's past. In presenting this diversity to the modern world they also reveal the challenges which await other local historians to take up the stories of their own areas. In doing so they contribute to the lively discipline that local history has become in recent years.

Maynooth Studies in Local History: Number 43

Coalisland, County Tyrone, in the Industrial Revolution, 1800–1901

Austin Stewart

FOUR COURTS PRESS

Set in 10pt on 12pt Bembo by
Carrigboy Typesetting Services, County Cork for
FOUR COURTS PRESS LTD
Fumbally Lane, Dublin 8, Ireland
e-mail: info@four-courts-press.ie
http://www.four-courts-press.ie
and in North America for
FOUR COURTS PRESS
c/o ISBS, 5824 N.E. Hassalo Street, Portland, OR 97213.

ISBN 1–85182–708–0

Printed in Ireland by
ColourBooks Ltd, Dublin

Acknowledgements

Many people have helped, in
writing this study. For th
staffs of the following libra
Maynooth, the National
Science library, the
Dublin Society li
Armagh; the W
and Cooks

In C
local
a

FIGURES

TABLES

many different ways, in researching and
eir courteous assistance I wish to thank the
ies and institutions: John Paul II Library, NUI,
Archives, Trinity College library, Queen's University
ublic Record Office of Northern Ireland, the Royal
rary, the Tomás Ó Fiaich Memorial Library and Archive,
estern Education and Library Board at Coalisland, Dungannon
own libraries, and the staff of the Heritage Centre, Coalisland.
alisland I am obliged to Jim Canning for his generous offer of time,
history, and hospitality. Anne Laverty of Stewartstown Historical Society,
d Tommy McIlvenna were there to warmly advise when requested.

My thanks to Robert Stewart, Snr. for a healthy scepticism – why Coalisland? His own love of place and sense of rootedness is probably a truer sentiment, and in no measure lies behind the initial stirring of the project.

Yvonne McCarthy, Virginia Keogh and Mary Behan offered computer assistance when needed. I am particularly grateful for the kind permission of Dr Michael Dillon to reproduce two OS maps from published work. And a word of appreciation to Dr Campbell Grant who was always upbeat and full of interest for a work in progress.

I am deeply obliged to my colleagues in the MA class in local history 1999–2001 for their genuine camaraderie and support. To Professor R.V. Comerford, Dr Colm Lennon, Dr Jacinta Prunta and the teaching staff of the Department of History my sincere thanks for their salutary guidance, inspiration and assistance, not least that of Ann Donoghue, Department secretary. To Dr Raymond Gillespie, my thesis supervisor, my warm thanks. A gifted teacher, Dr Gillespie through his guidance and comments generated an empathy that quickly grew into a remarkable and unmistakable feeling of being caught up in a huge adventure in local history. Janet, Colleen and Joe continued to look over my shoulder from time to time and nodded wisely. My grateful thanks to them for their interest and concern, not least about when it might all finish. I am grateful to the National Library of Ireland for permission to use figs. 5, 12, 14 and 15 from the Lawrence Collection.

Finally, my wholesome thanks and appreciation to my wife and helpmate, Jacinta, patient and supportive throughout the 'return to roots' afforded me in the pursuance of this study.

Introduction

For over two hundred years Coalisland town in east Tyrone was the inland port for Ulster's only substantial coalfield that extended over an area of almost thirteen square miles, the first reference to coal occurring in the Civil Survey of 1654. The industrial origins of the town can be traced back to 1729 where there were 'definite records of three coal pits, probably very small, supplying coal to "gentlemen" and "exporting" it to consumers on the shores of Lough Neagh'.[1] The town itself is partly located within the civil parishes of Donaghenry and Tullyniskan in the barony of middle Dungannon. It is four miles from the historic town of Dungannon and approximately seven miles south east of Cookstown. It lies three miles from the west shore of Lough Neagh (fig. 1). The river Torrent flows nearby into the river Blackwater and the Coalisland canal, first mooted in 1732, was finally completed in 1787.

There was no evidence at that time of any nucleated settlement but it is likely that the construction of the Coalisland canal in the middle of the eighteenth century was of prime importance in its later development. Prior

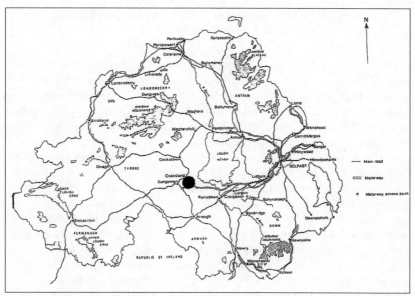

1 Location of Coalisland in Northern Ireland.
Source: P.A. Compton, *NI: a census atlas* (Dublin, 1978).

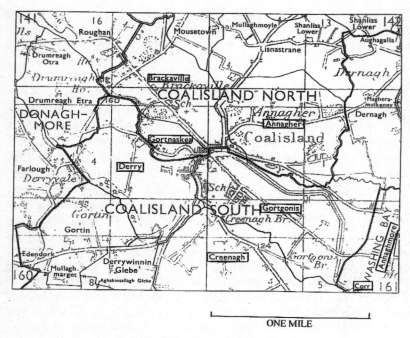

2 Coalisland townland region.
Source: OS, NI, Dungannon LGD, sheets 141, 142, 160, 161
scale 1:10,000, published 1974.

to the construction of the canal in 1744 the rural landscape in Coalisland was
probably 'dotted with farmer–miners' houses and small cabins'.[2] Eking out a
living in this landscape was not easy. The Ordnance Survey memoir in 1834
commented on the land around Coalisland in the northern part of the parish
of Tullyniskan as very poor, 'the hills being of a light gravelly nature and the
bottoms reclaimed or only partly reclaimed from bog'.[3] The average size of
a farm was eight acres and let at 18s. per acre, but the farms were too small to
'admit of any regular course of crops'. The local landlords were farmers or
'gentlemen bleachers' who charged £1 rent for cabins without land and £2
with a garden. These cabins were made of mud, stone or lime thatched and
they were not well finished. Most had bedsteads with straw or chaff beds and
there was no overcrowding. The population lived on a diet of potatoes and milk
or oatmeal. Weaving and labouring occupied a working man who could earn up
to £15 a year in wages. There were six public houses in Tullyniskan parish,
apparently well supported by the workers in the neighbouring collieries.[4]
According to the evidence presented to the Poor Inquiry of 1836 they were
a 'cause of great wretchedness'. The landscape west and north of Coalisland in

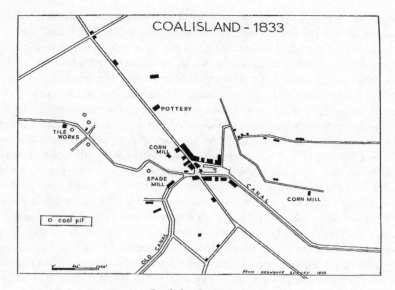

3 Coalisland town, 1833.
Source: M. Dillon, 'Coalisland: the evolution of an industrial landscape',
Studia Hibernica, 8 (1968), p. 80.

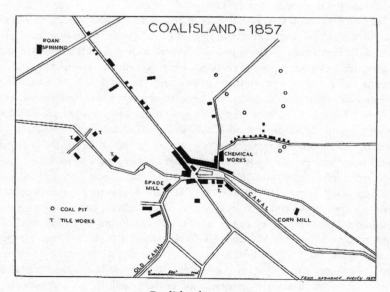

4 Coalisland town, 1857.
Source: M. Dillon, 'Coalisland: the evolution of an industrial landscape',
Studia Hibernica, 8 (1968), p. 82.

Donaghenry parish was only slightly better. The farms were still small but the soil was 'strong and good, resting upon a limestone rock'.[5] The house book of Coalisland town in the First Valuation in 1833[6] shows the housing stock to be of sturdier quality than that found in the surrounding country. Minimum rent was between £2 and £4 and 30 per cent of rents were between £4 and £10.

Against this background Coalisland's industrialization in the early nineteenth century proved more a regional than an urban phenomenon. The town was in a developmental stage and industrial activity was based more around the outlying townlands (fig.2) in the parishes of Tullyniskan, Donaghenry, Clonoe, Drumglass and Killyman, where coalmining and pottery works were carried on. In 1802 Coalisland's industrial base was at an all time low with the canal falling into disuse and physical access to the collieries in some doubt. It was only a temporary lull as over the next 25 years Coalisland's industrial activity revived with new initiatives in coalmining and the mushrooming of family pottery works. From the Ordnance Survey of 1833 (fig.3) it is clear how little coalmining, pottery or tile work was carried on in the immediate environs of Coalisland town. By 1857 these activities had substantially increased in the town area (fig. 4). Later in the century the factories and workshops in the town raised the industrial profile of Coalisland itself so that by 1901 the town economy was well advanced. This present study mirrors this evolving image of a regional economy in the early 1800s that becomes fully focused around Coalisland town at the end of the nineteenth century.

The dual source of Coalisland's early industrialism was found in its coalmines and the native clay that formed the basis of an indigenous pottery industry. In 1951 W.R. Hutchison in *Tyrone precinct*[7] devoted a chapter to the development of the collieries spanning three centuries. He was mainly concerned with their origins and fortunes in the eighteenth century. In 1980 W.A. McCutcheon revisited the collieries in chapter six of his seminal work *The industrial archaeology of Northern Ireland*.[8] The most important early nineteenth-century pre-Famine work on the development of Coalisland's industrial base was Richard Griffith's *Geological and mining surveys of the coal districts of the counties of Tyrone and Antrim*.[9] This present study draws on other contemporary sources including the Ordnance Survey memoirs for the parishes of Clonoe, Tullyniskan, and Drumglass. J.E. Portlock's *Report on the geology of the county of Londonderry and of parts of Tyrone and Fermanagh*, in 1843,[10] is a key contemporary source on the commercial potential of the mines and potteries and how they were worked. Later in the century E.T. Hardman's 'On the present state of coalmining in the county of Tyrone'[11] offers further insight on the stagnation of the collieries and their failure to act as an engine of industrial growth. Megan McManus points out that there was 'evidence of pottery making in some twenty different places in Ulster in the nineteenth century'.[12] Significantly, the evidence of the OS memoirs indicates that the Coalisland area, particularly in the townland of Creenagh, was the centre of this pottery industry. Portlock's report is negative on the coal economy but very positive about the potential of the Coalisland potteries to sustain enterprise and employment. In the nine-teenth century a number of potteries went out of business due to changing circumstances of the local economy as mechanised linen and weaving offered greater opportunities for work. Also, the success of the canal as a conduit for goods in and out of the area meant that cheap imported goods appeared and many local entrepreneurs felt that unfair rail freight charges worked against a reasonable return for their efforts.

Given Coalisland's industrial past it is remarkable how little attention it has received from historians seeking to discover the true nature of industrialism in Ireland in the nineteenth century. Writing at the end of an era in 1968, Michael Dillon drew attention to the fact that Coalisland's morphology was totally different to that of the linen towns of Ulster and noted that such a small settlement had an industrial character 'more reminiscent of the English midlands than Ireland.'[13] What is even more remarkable is that whatever was achieved in Coalisland in industrial terms in the nineteenth century was achieved by the Coalisland people themselves. Unlike in Co. Waterford where the enterprising Malcomson family ushered in industrial developments at Portlaw, or at Sion Mills in west Tyrone, where the Herdman family left their mark on an industrial village, Coalisland was blessed with no such benevolence. On the contrary, there is evidence to suggest that in the last quarter of the eighteenth century local land owners who received government money to develop industry in the Coalisland area found a better use for it in their own back pocket.[14] The much-trumpeted Ducart's canal link in 1777 from the coal pithead to the Coalisland basin resulted in one trial run and this to avoid being sued for misappropriation of government money.[15] Through the nine-teenth century the shadow of failure tended to dwarf Coalisland's industrial achievements, as much potential was never fully harnessed. This pamphlet sets out to explain why but more than that it seeks to set Coalisland's industrial past in the wider context of how the Industrial Revolution found its own nemesis in a rural enclave in east Tyrone.

The first chapter looks at Coalisland town before the Famine. It outlines the industrial potential that was there both in terms of the development of the collieries and the manufacture of pottery in the Coalisland region. The chapter sketches why this potential was never fully harnessed. The second chapter examines Coalisland town after the Famine and demonstrates that in addition to the extractive industries of coal and clay, the coming of Roan Spinning Mill (1848) and the Coalisland Weaving Company (1868) marked the emergence of the factory system in rural east Tyrone. The collieries are revisited where it becomes clear that by 1875 no one had properly addressed the structural weaknesses of under-resourcing, poor marketing, and adherence to obsolete methods of coal extraction. In the third chapter the 1901 census provides an important way of exploring the social structure of Coalisland. In

1981 D.S. Macneice in his important work on factory workers' housing used, to good effect, the census returns.[16] The title of his subsequent essay 'Industrial villages of Ulster, 1800–1900'[17] is, however, somewhat misleading insofar as if confined himself to a study of villages in east Ulster, Down and Armagh. Furthermore, the use of the term 'industrial' in his work is a synonym for linen enterprise and as such takes no cognizance of the reality of the multifaceted industrialism that was the experience of Coalisland during the nineteenth century. Coalisland's omission as an industrial settlement in this period needs to be addressed and this pamphlet, for the first time, does that. Macneice did reflect on the lack of analysis on small industrial communities 'in terms of religious breakdown, place of origin, age or mobility'[18] and the third chapter addresses this for the Coalisland community in 1901. Utilising enumerators' returns in the census it demonstrates how kinship, religion, housing and occupation shaped demography and social structure.

5 Coalisland port, *c*.1900.

1. Coalisland before the Famine

'A flourishing trading village'[1]

Coalisland town in east Tyrone in the nineteenth century was a hub of industrial activity, a phenomenon due to a complex deposit of natural resources, coal and clay, not found together in such quantities anywhere else.[2] Coalisland's first industrial phase, based on the mining of coal, began in the early part of the eighteenth century but by 1800 it was clear that this first industrial phase had run its course. McEvoy in 1802 wrote that there were five coal pits working there but the level of technology employed meant that there was no fire engine used in raising the coal.[3] He furthermore observed that the canal at Coalisland, gateway to outside markets, was choked with weeds and that the approaches to the collieries were in a ruinous state. This suggests that the coal then extracted was utilized for local purposes only and Coalisland was experiencing an economic downturn. We can further surmise that the lack of investment and initiatives necessary to work the more productive seams meant that only surface and inferior coal was mined. By 1812 the optimism of previous generations that Coalisland had the potential to be a Dublin coal merchant's Mecca was set to naught when barges conveying English coal plied their way into the canal basin unloading their cargo for distribution there and beyond to the hinterland (fig. 5).[4]

The economic downturn did not last and there was a veritable renaissance in the coal industry in Coalisland, which was to peak between 1830 and 1850. Out of this renaissance there developed a number of industries that included the manufacture of tiles, bricks, spades, shovels, sulphur and sulphuric acid and above all the development of pottery earthenware and fireclay goods. The communications system, particularly the Tyrone Navigation, was a huge enabling factor in sustaining this economic growth for the middle years of the century. The physical appearance of the town was clearly defined in the First Valuation map in 1833.[5] The house book[6] that accompanied this map shows Coalisland located in the townland of Brackaville. It also marginally extended into the adjacent townlands of Gortgonis and Gortnaskea in the parish of Tullyniskan. Gortgonis townland had seven people living in the town proper and seven more were described as 'living in the country', where James and William Lecky had their spade factory. The wealthiest part of town, judging by the valuations placed on the property, were those houses, stores and offices found in Gortgonis alongside the canal basin. Lecky's premises were described in the house book as the 'best part of town for a shop'. By modern standards it was a relatively small settlement but every reference in the house book was to that of 'town', indicating a place apart. Coalisland's empire was initially built on coal and extractive industries and later mechanized industry and through this it had no problem distinguishing itself from its hinterland.

In 1837 Samuel Lewis offered a snapshot of this evolving landscape.[7] He described it as a flourishing trading village in the centre of the Tyrone coalfield with 184 houses. Surprisingly, the 1841 census four years later only recorded 103 houses perhaps pointing up a certain fluidity in establishing exact boundaries in an area that was fast expanding. Lewis estimated that the local collieries covered an area of 12 square miles and it was originally thought that the coalfields could keep Dublin supplied for 60 odd years.[8] The government in 1744 had provided money to build a canal between Coalisland and Lough Neagh in order to give easy access to Newry and onward passageway by sea to Dublin. It was intended that the canal would intersect the entire coalfield of east Tyrone. This did not happen. Even so, Lewis judged Coalisland to be a place of considerable trade, with 35 large lighters, or barges, making frequent coasting voyages to Dublin and Scotland.[9]

In 1831 extensive ironworks, forges, and plating mills had been established. Just outside the area the manufacture of spades and edge tools were to the fore in Oghran and Newmills. In 1834 firebricks and crucibles were manufactured by two entrepreneurs from Stourbridge in Worcester and according to Lewis most of the manufactured articles were sent to London or Liverpool.[10] Also at this time in Coalisland there was a pottery and a flourmill where 2,000 tons of wheat were annually ground for the Belfast market. There were ample bleach-greens where 20,000 pieces of linen were annually finished for the English market.[11] The Coalisland canal basin was the centre of all this activity around which there were warehouses and granary yards. Several wealthy merchants like George Sloan, James and William Lecky, George Wilcocks, and James T. Caruth had valuable properties and stores in the village. The exports from the village were coal, spades, shovels, firebricks, fire-clay, crucibles, earthenware, linen cloth, wheat, oats, flour; imports included timber, iron, salt, slates, and glass via the canal. In Lewis' account from 1837 we are conscious of an 'outside world' and the targeting of markets in Dublin, Belfast, London, Liverpool and Scotland. This upbeat account in Lewis concerning the Coalisland economy was further reinforced by the Poor Inquiry in 1836 when evidence was sought concerning the economy of the area.[12] The Coalisland businessman Jonathan Pike found it hard to know where there was unemployment in the parish. He considered there was so much work around between labouring and manufacturing that it was hard to see how anyone could be idle. However, in a salutary reminder that a rising tide does not raise all boats, the parish priest of Donaghenry, Francis Gahan, reckoned there were 200 employed in the parish but only 16 were in constant employment. They all lived on potatoes and buttermilk and their clothing was coarse.

The basis of this apparent prosperity was the Coalisland collieries located to both the north and south of the town. In 1829 Richard Griffith, mining engineer to the Royal Dublin Society, published his estimates of these deposits. Coals found there 'are easily ignited, flame briskly, and burn swiftly, leaving a considerable residuum of white or greyish white ashes'.[13] There were two types of coal: large coal which was used for domestic purposes and there was the smaller coal that was used for burning lime and bricks. This latter coal from the colliery was taken by land carriage and marketed up to twenty miles away. The larger screened coal was sold at 13s. 4d. per ton and the quality of the smaller coal dictated prices ranging between 5s. to 8s. 4d. a ton. Most of the coal was consumed locally and Griffith reckoned that only a sixth was shipped out of the area on lighters to Portadown, Randalstown, Ballyronan and neighbouring ports on Lough Neagh.[14] For the years 1840 and 1841 coal sold at Annagher colliery amounted to 19,154 tons of which, 3,081 tons were large coal, and 16,073 tons small. We may deduce from this that the commercial use of coal in the burning of lime and bricks took precedence over its use as a domestic fuel or more likely large coal was not there to be mined in significant quantities. Griffith employed 77 men and boys in his mine. Fifty of them were employed underground as coal cutters, and hurriers. The rest worked on the surface.

Griffith's account of the system of working at the Coalisland colliery is important as it raises the question of whether the collieries could ever have been a viable enterprise to match the sanguine expectations of Dublin and Belfast merchant classes. The coal in the Annagher mine, which Griffith managed, was described as resting on a 'stratum of light grey fireclay, which is very soft, and consequently forms a bad floor for the coal workings ... this fire-clay is much used in the manufacture of fire bricks and fire tiles, both of which are of excellent quality, and equal to any imported from England or Scotland.'[15] Because of the soft and incoherent nature of the strata great difficulty was experienced in propping up the mine shafts as the fire clay on the floor of the shafts was prone to swelling and heaving. Yet despite these difficulties railways of wrought iron were laid in the main levels though daily repairs were necessary to preserve them in working order.[16] Raising the coal out of the mine was done by use of horse gins. Steam power was not a consideration because the mine was not worked extensively enough to warrant such expense. With the best efforts the levels in the mine could only be preserved for a period of two years and under these circumstances 'the cost of erecting engine-houses, steam engines, and setting up pumps every two years, would be much more expensive in the aggregate than employing six horses every twenty four hours at each pit'.[17] Griffith argued that the operational practice in his mine was the norm in the area and managed to make a 'small return to the proprietors'.[18] When Portlock was compiling his report on the geology of Tyrone and Fermanagh in 1842–3 he had visited the Annagher coal mine and he thought that the lay-out of the place was 'rude and unfavourable', and the buildings were very limited.[19] He felt that greater marketing strategy on both Griffith's part and that of the Hibernian Company would have yielded greater results. In particular, he felt that since coal was sent out of the area up to a distance of 20 miles it would have made sense 'if the proprietors adopted the principle of forming depots for their coal at all the chief towns within a reasonable distance, and then contracted for its transmission to them'.[20]

The Hibernian Mining Company, to the south of the town, did bring a new professionalism to coal extraction by introducing more sophisticated equipment at the Drumglass colliery. By 1829 coal pits were in operation in the townlands of Killybrackey, Lurgaboy, Farlough, Creenagh, Gortnaskea, Brackaville and Annagher. By 1834 the Annagher coalfield was not currently worked because the roof was too soft and there were difficulties in procuring supporting timbers in sufficient number.[21] At Killybrackey in 1834, two steam engines of 70- and 30-horsepower, the property of the Hibernian Mining Company were in use. The larger engine was employed clearing the mine of water and the smaller one raised the coal from a depth of 128 yards.[22] At the time that Portlock was compiling his report in the early 1840s the overseer and manager of the Drumglass pits was Edward Sinclair. The Lewin mine was the only one in operation and Sinclair's description gives an excellent insight as to the mining operation there.[23] Sinclair was progressive and saw the need to introduce machinery and techniques as were in general use in the north of England. There were 104 men and boys employed underground in this mine and Sinclair further relates

> The youngest boy is ten years old, the oldest man forty-six. Ten hours is considered a shift or day's work here, but as the greatest portion of the work is piece-work, and as we have more men than are fully employed, the majority of them do not work more than nine hours. There are fourteen surface labourers, 2 engine men, 2 stokers, 1 carpenter, 2 sawyers, 2 smiths, and they are paid as follows: – the surface labourers (screeners, &c.) 1s. 2d. a-day, smith 2s. 6d., carpenter 2s. 6d., pair of sawyers 4s. 6d., enginemen 2s., and stokers 1s. 2d. The day's work is twelve hours in summer, out of which an hour and a half must be deducted for breakfast and dinner, and eleven hours in winter, with three-quarters of an hour allowed for breakfast and dinner. And besides these payments about £3 weekly are expended in paying for carrying coals to lighters at Coalisland and Moy, and about twenty carmen are also employed in leading coals to various places and bringing pit timber.[24]

Sinclair does point out that there were more men on the mine than were fully employed and there was also expensive equipment in the possession of the company that was grossly under-utilized. There were a number of engines lying idle:[25] one 90-horse condensing engine at Drumglass old colliery, a 24-horse power high pressure engine at Clonoe colliery and in the company stores were a 35-horse power condensing engine, a horse power engine and two double-horse whim-gins. As a result of this inefficiency coal sales at Drumglass and Lurgaboy fell from a peak of 23,635 tons in 1833 to 14,102 tons in 1837.

Portlock in the 1840s considered the mines at Drumglass to be well worked and that the seams were in no way exhausted but, as in the Annagher mine, he cavilled 'that no means are adopted to extend the demand and augment the supply'.[26] The failure to market properly meant that the expensive machinery of the Hibernian Company was not utilised and there was no concerted effort to reduce mining costs to make the mining enterprise competitive. Capital was squandered because of the necessity to make frequent new bores due to the broken nature of the coal seams. By the 1840s the challenge to the collieries was patent. The increased use of local clays in the making of bricks, pottery, and fire-clay goods, along with the general expansion of the Ulster linen trade meant that the demand for coal increased. Potential development for the collieries was never greater but the future of coal at the collieries was never assured. There was no one prepared to sink the capital required to bring British mining technologies to rural east Tyrone.[27] Forty years later matters had greatly deteriorated. By 1872 when Hardman issued his report on coalmining in Tyrone he referred to the style of mining in Coalisland as both 'antique and timid' and went on to say

> For at least a century, the coal has been continuously wrought, innumerable pits having been opened and a large quantity of fuel removed, without, however, benefiting to any appreciable extent any person concerned, save perhaps the owners of the royalties.[28]

He found it extraordinary that 'the coal is taken down entirely by means of a pick. The variety used is a short straight head, with a handle of 30 inches. With this the miner very slightly holes the seam and then hews it down. In this way much of the coal is spoiled the greater portion becoming slack'.[29] McCutcheon summed it up:

> The output of coal from such collieries was negligible in comparison with what it had been half a century previously. The great expectations of earlier decades had not been fulfilled and gradually the extensive underground workings had been allowed to close up with pressure from the soft clays often forming the sides, roof or floor, being replaced by ephemeral, shallow pits which answered an immediate purpose but held no prospect of planned development.[30]

The coalmines were clearly central to the Coalisland area's prosperity before the Famine. Also during the period Coalisland generated a reputation as an area where the making of coarse pottery ware was a key industry. In 1802 McEvoy wrote that 'the best pottery in the country and perhaps in the kingdom is within a mile of Coalisland on the road to Verner's ferry in the barony of Dungannon. Here are manufactured all sorts of rough crockery ware, fire-bricks and tiles for malt and oat kilns, of as good quality as any imported.'[31] The 1834 six-inch Ordnance Survey map located nine sites in the Coalisland area as places where pottery manufacture was carried on.[32] It is clear that the most extensive potteries were carried on in the parish of Tullyniskan and particularly in the townland of Creenagh. The Ordnance Survey memoirs help paint a fuller picture of the pottery industry at this time. McManus' account remarks on the paucity of detail in the relevant memoir dealing with Clonoe parish which states that only 'pottery ware of a coarse description and bricks of an inferior quality are manufactured in the southern parts of the parish, but only to a trifling extent'.[33] Yet, elsewhere in the same memoir significant reference is indeed made to Meenagh townland where 'potters clay of the best description and in great abundance is found at the depth of 20 yards from the surface. It is in some places 49 feet in thickness and is suitable for all the purposes of fine pottery ware, being thought by some not to be inferior to the Staffordshire clays. The bed extends over a great portion of the townland, in some places cropping out to the surface.'[34] The reference to the potteries in the memoir for Tullyniskan parish indicates that there was a tile industry in Derry townland; and in Creenagh and Gortgonis townlands there were several small potteries with at least four located in Gortgonis, all surrounding the town of Coalisland. The memoir remarks on how manpower was deployed 'in these potteries 7 persons are employed at 1 spinning wheel'.[35] The spinner received 2s. 3d. for his day's work and the labourers about 10d.[36] Portlock in the 1840s described this spinning wheel as a wheel turned by a handcrank. The memoir goes on to say how the pottery pieces are sold, where the clay and lead ore for glazing is sourced '60 pieces are sold for about 30s. or 35s. according to the season. Red clay was usually found in the potter's own land, white clay is purchased at 4s. 2d. per ton. For the lead ore used in glazing they send to Belfast or Dublin'.[37] Portlock in his report in 1843 was upbeat about the potential of the Coalisland potteries. The clay for earthenware was widespread locally in depths of up to 30 feet deep that the manufacture of tiles and draining tiles could be greatly extended.[38] This was beginning to happen. In Killyman parish, beside Coalisland, Robinson's pottery was producing 8,000 tiles. In the townland of Brackaville in Coalisland a Mr. Newburn was reviving an abandoned pottery and was producing 4,000 flooring tiles, 400 ridge tiles at 3d. each and 5,000 firebricks. Other pottery works were Kilpatrick's at Drumenagh in Killyman parish where 6,000 draining tiles, were made and sold to the local landlord. The manufacture of draining tiles seemed to be the market leader at several Coalisland establish-ments.[39] Yet despite this activity Portlock was not impressed by the failure of entrepreneurs to become involved in more-up-to-date methods in tile manufacture. He referred in particular to the invention of a simple tile-making machine costing £45 wherewith two men and one boy could easily make 500 draining tiles in one hour.[40] Again, as in the development of the collieries, there did not seem to be the will or the capital available to take pottery development to a new level.

Given this rather unusual economic base, the population of Coalisland in the nineteenth century should have had a rather unusual history also. The Co. Tyrone population at the start of the nineteenth century was still expanding and was to peak in 1831 with an increase of 16 per cent on 1821.[41] The following ten years saw an increase of only 3 per cent. For the rest of the century Tyrone's population, through emigration and declining birth rate fell. The county lost 35 per cent of its population between 1821 and 1891. However, the population of Coalisland town in east Tyrone differed dramatically from the county pattern. Coalisland trebled its population between 1821 and 1891. It saw a population increase of 39 per cent between 1841 and 1851 (Table 1) and it went on increasing during the rest of the century with a slight dip in the 1860s. This population growth was sustained by the expansion of coalmining between 1830 and 1850 and further fuelled by the economic activities of the potteries and small manufacturing industries. Later in the century, as the domestic linen industry went into terminal decline in the county, Coalisland rose to the challenge by adapting to mechanised linen production.

Table 1. Parish/Town population, 1821–91

Year	Donaghenry parish	% change	Tullyniskan parish	% change	Coalisland	% change
1821	4,853		3,536			
1831	5,384	+ 10.9	4,102	+ 16		
1841	5,673	+ 5.4	4,106	+ 0.1	451	
1851	4,820	- 1.5	3,474	- 15.4	627	+ 39
1861	4,749	- 1.5	3,203	- 7.8	661	+ 5.4
1871	4,246	- 10.6	3.070	- 4.2	598	- 9.5
1881	3,828	- 9.8	2,911	- 5.2	677	+ 13.2
1891	3,351	- 12.5	2,437	- 16.3	785	+ 16

Source: Censuses of population, 1821–91

During the nineteenth century the village and later the town of Coalisland was located partly in the parish of Tullyniskan and partly in the parish of Donaghenry in east Tyrone. A footnote in the 1821 Census refers to the section of the village in Donaghenry as containing 35 houses and 176 inhabitants. No mention was made of that part of the village that rested in Tullyniskan parish. This omission probably reflects the unsatisfactory nature of the 1821 Census.[42] The 1831 census is even more unsatisfactory in that no mention at all is made of Coalisland as a separate entity. Its population structure was absorbed into the population returns for both the parishes of Donaghenry and Tullyniskan.[43] It is not until the 1841 census that the two parts of Coalisland are represented as distinct entities. In the 1841 census the population of Coalisland in Tullyniskan parish represented almost 40 per cent of the total town population and this trend continued during the following four decades. For 1821 we have only the Donaghenry population segment. Yet, by applying the pattern suggested by these percentages backwards (and bearing in mind the underestimation in these early census returns) it is reasonable to assume that the proportion of Coalisland population in Tullyniskan in 1821 may conservatively represent 40 per cent of the total. This would give a population of 246 in the 1821 census. This would also mean that in the 20 years to 1841 the population of Coalisland increased more than 80 per cent and on the 10-year period to 1851 the population increased another 39 per cent. (Table 1). The reasons for the surge in population are not hard to find since it coincides with the peak years in coal production between 1830 and 1850.[44] With the release of working capital tied up during the Napoleonic wars there was speculation, already entertained in the latter part of the eighteenth century, that Coalisland could become the epicentre of an Irish coal industry in the north of Ireland. Since 1818 the mining engineer of the Royal Dublin Society, Richard Griffith, had been centrally advocating the possibilities of such enterprise. In 1829 he wrote that 'at present the Tyrone coal District is one of the most important in Ireland; it is situated in the midst of a country inhabited by an industrious and manufacturing population'.[45] During these years the three factors of local supplies of coal, surface clays and ease of com-munication in and out of the area via the canal gave rise to a host of ancillary industry. These industries included the manufacture of tiles and bricks; pottery, earthenware and fireclay goods; spades and shovels, sulphur and sulphuric acid.

In the pre-Famine years Coalisland as a settlement remained small. In part this reflects the small-scale basis of the local economy despite an appearance of industrialisation in the mines and potteries. The evidence from the Ordnance Survey Memoirs and Portlock show that the pottery business generally had been worked with small pockets of manpower in a rural setting or townland. To a great extent the industry fulfilled Mendels[46] basic features for a theory of 'proto-industrialization'. The main feature is the growth of a rural industry involving peasant participation in some sort of handicraft. The industry may provide income supplement to agricultural activity or it could be a full time family occupation.[47] The Coalisland pottery craft operated in this way. The theory also stresses that the market for the goods produced should be outside the area. For Mendels this was an important point distinguishing it from 'petty industry' which over time supplied local needs. Coalisland exported finished pottery pieces through the canal and met this condition. The theory of proto-industrialization seeks to demonstrate and explain a stage in industrial development that, more often than not, historically falters and fizzles out before the development has achieved full potential. The Coalisland potteries and indeed the collieries are a case in point. Early industrialization in Coalisland, as its name suggests, was based on extractive industries. First, there was coal, then clay. The second chapter will demonstrate how later in the century non-extractive industries also played their part. A mechanised linen industry was established in 1848. This was Roan Spinning Mill located in the townland of Brackaville. In 1868 the Coalisland Weaving Company was established and together these industries were to mark the emergence of the factory system in a rural enclave of east Tyrone. The geographic and physical conditions for this 'take off' were not hard to find. The area had a suitable and adequate supply of water, a damp climate, a huge acreage yield in flax, and a well-established canal system offering ease of transport. In addition, there were local supplies of coal as a source of power and for building infrastructure there was an abundant supply of brick, stone, sand and lime. Above all there was a huge depth of indigenous human capital and expertise in weaving and spinning. All this was to change the face of industry in the Coalisland region as a new economic order, reflected in the emergence of the mass market, took root.

2. Coalisland after the Famine

'a wretched tumbledown village, in which nothing seems to go well'[1]

The collieries and the potteries helped to shape the pre-Famine economic and social structure of Coalisland yet by the 1870s, surprisingly, Coalisland's industrial base had not significantly advanced. Most damning was Hardman's 1872 assessment of the place where 'instead of being a thriving town, full of life and industry, with such manufacturers as the presence of a coalfield might naturally create, is a wretched tumbledown village, in which nothing seems to go well. It contains three or four mills and tile works, and the ruins of former mismanagement'.[2] The foundations for future development were in place on the eve of the Famine. The First Valuation map of 1834 (fig. 6) and Griffith's Valuation map of 1859 (fig. 7) show that the town expanded, primarily through massive subdivision of earlier holdings, with the area covered by the town remaining substantially the same over the course of a generation. The clays that formed the raw material for the potteries, in evidence in the first Ordnance Survey map, continued to be mined and the economic importance of the potteries remained as the century progressed. The markets for the finished product did change and Coalisland adapted accordingly. The Burns family from Creenagh townland, renowned for their earthenware goods in the earlier part of the century, concentrated on the manufacture of heavier pottery, especially fire-clay pipes from 1870 onwards.[3] In the town itself the Devlin family in 1890 established a similar business opposite the canal basin which was subsequently acquired by the Corr family. After the Famine a number of potteries went out of business, possibly because of the change in the domestic economy wrought by the coming of the factory system to the area. There was a greater reliance on cheap imported goods and many small entrepreneurs had problems with what they considered unfair rail freight charges. Despite the high output implicit in Portlock's account, potteries may not have been as profitable an enterprise as they were earlier in the century. Again, because they were family businesses, family circumstances did change and people moved on. Two contrasting cases are cited to illustrate the point.

The first case is that of Dan Devlin who started a pottery business in Coalisland in the early 1870s manufacturing all kind of stoneware, glazed pipes and terracotta goods. He built the plant from scratch, fitting it out with the most up-to-date machinery and his pottery goods went all over the North. In 1886 he went bankrupt and a workforce of 50 men left the town with a loss to the local economy of £100 a fortnight. He argued he could not

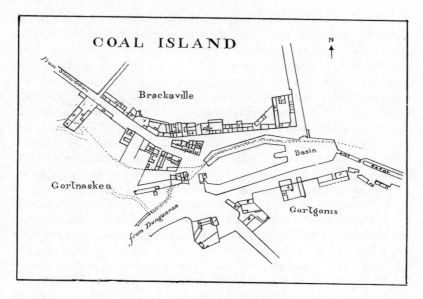

6 Coalisland, 1833, First Valuation map.

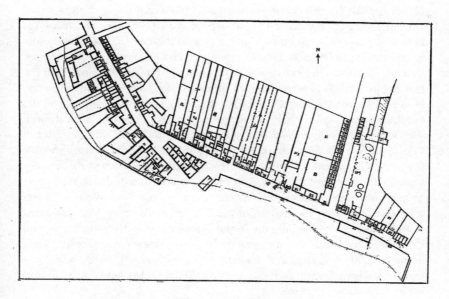

7 Coalisland, 1859, Griffith's Valuation map.

compete with cheap imports from England and Scotland because of excessive rail freight charges. He told a Parliamentary Select Committee in 1885[4] that because his Coalisland plant consumed 200 tons of coal a month he could only obtain half of this coal locally. The rest he had to import. This was expensive in contrast to the manufacturers of pottery in Scotland who had ample supplies of coal on their doorstep and were facilitated by reasonable freight charges. This allowed them to dominate the pottery market throughout Ulster. In Coalisland pottery terms Devlin's operation was a large set-up. A different kind of pottery works that was small-scale and family run is cited in McManus.[5] In 1858 Joseph Kilpatrick had a pottery valued in Griffith's Valuation at £3 in Ballynakelly, another valued at £2 in Annaghmore. He owned a pub, a forge and twenty-one acres of land. At the time of his death in 1872 he owned another pottery at Drumenagh. In his will he left his wife Leticia a house, farm, cattle, crops, and a boat. His daughter Mary and Elizabeth were both left pottery works, and his son John was left 30 acres of land and when he reached 21 years he was to inherit 'The line' pottery and all its attachments. The potteries did not survive long after Joseph Kilpatrick. In 1879, seven years after his death, the pottery at Drumenagh was in ruins; Ballynakelly and Annaghmore ceased operations respectively in 1883 and 1906. In contrast, the Burns family in Creenagh townland had a long association with the pottery industry and continued operating well into the twentieth century.

By comparison to this stagnation in traditional pre-Famine industry in Coalisland the population of the town continued to grow in the years after 1851 in contrast to the decline in Co. Tyrone as a whole. Since the traditional industrial base could not support such a growth it is necessary to consider the economic change which made such population growth possible. One important area of growth was the expansion of the linen industry. By 1861 over half the families of Coalisland were involved in handicrafts, trades or manufacturing. However, the basis for this was not rural domestic industry characteristic of the early nineteenth century but the emergence of a factory system in Coalisland. This was in no small measure due to the opening of Roan Spinning Mill in Coalisland in 1848. The coming of the Coalisland Weaving Factory in 1868 was to further boost job prospects. It is significant that when this factory started out there were over 500 applications for jobs, and of that number over 90 per cent described themselves as either handloom weavers or hand spinners,[6] reflecting the demise of most domestic industry with increased factory production. The only dip in the Coalisland population in the second half of the nineteenth century came in the 1860s. This is somewhat surprising in the context of weaving and the linen trade. It suggests a mobile workforce that sought greater returns elsewhere as the linen trade found a new lease of life as the decade progressed.

Roan Spinning Mill on the outskirts of the town was well poised to capitalise on the demise of the cotton industry when the American Civil War erupted in 1862. Initially, it was thought this would bring disaster on the linen trade because of the fall-off in demand from a market that consumed so large a proportion of Irish linen goods. Instead of disaster the opposite happened. Increased demand for linen goods of all kinds was experienced, especially cloth suitable for clothing. Demand for coarse goods soared and by the end of the year prices had advanced. The linen trade experienced great prosperity when the American Civil War was ongoing and the cotton trade collapsed. This prosperity continued to the end of 1866 but with the revival of cotton in 1867 a reaction set in. A linen trade circular referred to the 'disastrous events' in 1867 where 'neither merchant nor manufacturer was accorded those rewards which the investment of capital and the exercise of industry should have secured.'[7] As prices dropped further raw materials were affected and two years later spinners were curtailing their production by one-third either by short time or stoppage of machinery.[8] Significantly, it was at this critical point in the economic cycle that the Coalisland Weaving Factory came into existence in 1868. Prosperity in the linen business did return early in the 1870s, and this upturn did help the factory to root itself. This economic resurgence coincided with a population jump in Coalisland in the 1870s and 1880s. In contrast, there was a haemorrhage of population from the surrounding rural districts of Donaghenry and Tullyniskan, where population fell by 15 per cent between 1861 and 1871,[9] another 15 per cent between 1871 and 1881,[10] and an enormous decline of 29 per cent between 1881 and 1891.[11] One possibility for this was that people were moving to the town; another possibility was increased migration out of the area. It is reasonable to presume that the census figures reflect a movement from the countryside to the town. As the century progressed and the linen factories grew in Coalisland, coalmining in the area became less important as an economic activity.

In the twenty-year period 1871–91 the number of coalminers dropped by 41 per cent with the largest decline in the industry coming in the 1880s. In 1881 there were fewer numbers employed in the Coalisland collieries than were employed in a single mine managed by Richard Griffith in the 1830s. This was not due to a lack of coal. E. T. Hardman's report of 1872 wrote of the Coalisland collieries that the quantity of coal mined up to the early 1870s was not large compared to the potential deposits that awaited 'the enterprising miner'.[12] One million tons of coal had been removed but there were at least 12 million tons untouched. At the Drumglass colliery, lying near Dungannon, about one and a half million tons had been removed and of known resources four and a half million had yet to be mined. Hardman further estimated that the available tonnage of coal from the district including the possibility of unknown resources might have amounted to 32 million tons. Despite this there was 'the most extraordinary apathy' in getting it out. The irony was that the Coalisland coalfield possessed ten types of coal, many of which were 'much thicker than seams often worked with advantage at a great depth in England.'[13] It was eminently situated as a centre of supply being within reasonable distance of Dungannon, Cookstown, and other manufacturing towns. The canal connected Coalisland with Lough Neagh and goods could be conveyed cheaply to Portadown, Antrim, Lurgan, and from there onwards to Belfast. Yet, notwithstanding all this, Coalisland experienced 'company after company breaking up in disgust, and the workings of private individuals becoming fewer every year'.[14] There were two reasons for this. First, there was a reluctance to invest large sums of money on the chance of hitting on a good mine and secondly, the controlling influence of the indigenous workforce.

The miners themselves dictated in no uncertain fashion how the mines were to be worked. The days of a pit were numbered 'for if a trifling roll or "trouble" is met with, the miners lose heart and abandon the work'.[15] Miners in Coalisland had a grave dislike of deep pits and argued to their mine owners that coals were better worked, and more cheaply, by sinking shallow pits on them than by working long levels. As the owners appeared to depend entirely on the 'practical knowledge' of the working colliers, they continued to spend the money that one shaft had earned in putting down another one. The owners compensated for this backward exploration by asking extremely high prices for the little coal that was produced.[16] This dominance of the miners' 'practical knowledge' meant that they never dreamt of extending their shafts into lower workings or to look for coal when the upper seam of coal had been exhausted or failed. One of the positive aspects of the surface mining carried on was that there continued to be very few accidents in the pits. Often, whenever there was an incident it was conveyed as a non-event. At Annagher colliery when John Donaghy employed as a 'hurrier' thought that the cage by which the coal was brought to the top had arrived, he consequently pushed the vehicle of coal on, as he thought, to it; but the cage not being there the 'bogey', as it was called, fell into the 'sump' and he after it. He escaped almost unhurt.[17] Furthermore, the 'practical knowledge' of the miner was also found wanting in the choice of ground to be mined where a 'rule of thumb' method of mining seemed to dominate. This led to pits being sunk perilously close to large faults which could never be expected to make any reasonable return.[18] At the time it was commonplace to believe that the coals lay in sets of distinct basins or 'pounds' and that a fault indicated the dying out of the out-cropping of the seam under work. Hardman's view was that this was an erroneous and mistaken belief and was 'not confined to the illiterate'.[19] The net consequence was a coalfield 'honey-combed with the most palpable of failures',[20] resulting in the most dramatic and tragic failure of the Congo colliery in 1895.

Over the next 20 years Hardman's optimistic assessment of the potential of the Coalisland coalfield continued to inspire but usually with mixed results, reflecting the passing of the importance of coal in the local economy. The immediate response to his report was to galvanize local merchants in Dungannon and Coalisland to come together to form the Tyrone Coalmining Company (hereafter TMC) which was incorporated on 17 September 1873.[21]

Two of the main shareholders were Thomas Dickson, a linen manufacturer in Dungannon, and James Brown from Donaghmore, a hamlet two miles from Coalisland. Others joined them, notably Benjamin Whitworth, a London merchant. Minor shareholders were William Wilson of the Coalisland Spinning Mill and John Stevenson from the spade factory. For a short time extensive coalmining operations were attempted across a range of up to twenty townlands in the Coalisland area. The venture was ill-fated from the beginning, trading unsuccessfully and forced into liquidation in 1877.[22] Silas Evans, a Belfast stockbroker and the secretary to the company, was appointed liquidator.

Local merchants Dickson and Brown were bitterly disappointed at the turn of events. They did a deal with the liquidator and set about forming a new company called the Dungannon Mining Company. This new company purchased the interest of TMC and resumed mining operations.[23] The sum of money agreed for the purchase was £7,000 but only a down payment of £3,000 was made. Oddly, Silas Evan, the liquidator now became secretary to the newly formed Dungannon company on a salary of £50 per annum.[24] After the failure of the TMC it became increasingly difficult to drum up interest in the new company. Significantly, Coalisland merchants Wilson and Stevenson did not participate. The main shareholders came from outside. They were four Manchester merchants, a London merchant and local entrepreneurs Dickson and Brown. The company traded for a few years up to 1879 and the minute book records board meetings taking place in Manchester. It became clear that the affairs of the Dungannon Mining Company were to be administered from afar and in an increasingly laissez faire fashion. The liquidator now became anxious to seek the remaining £4,000 of the purchase price. The shareholders in the new company refused to pay it. At one point they threatened to wash their hands of the whole business by handing the mining properties back and walking away.[25] Eventually, on 30 June 1879 agreement was reached, the Dungannon Mining Company paid £3,500 in full discharge of the liquidator's claim. Despite this the new company did little. No board meetings were held between 1879 and 1881. Active mining operations ceased and the works were practically dormant. Most important of all the company's money appeared to have run out.[26] The local shareholders Dickson and Brown, became alarmed that the venture was about to fail. They sought to rescue it by doing a deal with the other shareholders. They agreed to pay the rents and royalties and to work the shallow mines for local consumption. This was the situation until the arrival in the 1890s of a new Manchester initiative to attempt to rejuvenate the collieries. Then, an unheard of £40,000 was to be invested in machinery and equipment.

Optimism about the potential of coal deposits continued to generate 'black gold' fever. Coalisland and its environs by the early 1890s were criss crossed with a series of underground tunnelling. Any new venture was eagerly reported upon. Local entrepreneurs Messrs Corr and McNally opened a coal pit in the townland of Gortgonis in July 1891 giving employment to a considerable number.[27] Improvement came slowly, if at all. Hardman in 1872 had cavilled at the absence of the 'banking of coal '.[28] Coal was merely turned out as it was wanted. This meant that it was normal practice for a string of carts to wait in line for hours on end at the collieries, and for the end carts to return without a coal load. By contrast, in the early 1890s firms like the Mid-Ulster Coal and Trading Company stock piled imports of English and Scotch coal and advertised distribution centres in Tyrone at Caledon, Aughnacloy, Ballygawley, Clogher, Fivemiletown. The company further offered quotations for wagonloads of coal from the ships' side at Warrenpoint.[29] Around Coalisland royalties continued to be let. The townlands of Drumreagh (Upper and Lower), Derry, Brackaville, Gortnaskea were described as being rich in coal seams varying from three to five feet in thickness of an excellent quality covering 900 acres in total.[30] They belonged to Lord Charlemont and Sir Nathaniel A. Staples who were prepared to enter into negotiations for letting the rights to raise coal there. A significant detail in the prospectus for these letting rights referred to a mining shaft in one townland servicing lower seams of coal in sur-rounding townlands. This suggests that there was an attempt to move away from the traditional shallow surface mining commented upon by Hardman in 1872.[31] If this was so it was hardly because of a change in mindset or 'practical knowledge' of the indigenous workforce. Rather, it was the increasing number of visits from outside entrepreneurs. Many of these represented colliery companies in Scotland. Typically, they would come initially to make inquiries and examine the locale about Coalisland with a view to opening a coal pit and return to Scotland to consult colleagues.[32] It was clear that the fate and destiny of the Tyrone collieries would now rest with external agencies.

In July 1894 there was exciting news that renewed exploration in the Congo townland had struck coal 200 yards from the surface. The new company formed to undertake the exploration had done so in the belief that it was a speculative and hazardous exercise. The *Tyrone Courier* was in no doubt that the success was due to the 'indomitable pluck and perseverance of the present company over any other that had tried it.'[33] The Belfast newspapers were always keen to entertain notions of El Dorado in the Tyrone coalfields. These were notions that a burgeoning Belfast merchant class found easy to flirt with. What better way to enhance commercial self-image and attract inward investment than to believe that the satellite fields of Tyrone harboured potential bounty? Often this belief was reinforced by denigrating how the coalfields were worked in the past. The *Belfast Newsletter* wrote of the history of coal mining in Coalisland

> as a record of partial if not entire failure, unproductive effort not a result of the character of the area but as one of injudicious, ill-advised, ill-conducted operations and the lack of sufficient capital to pursue the operations to a successful and remunerative issue.[34]

The paper now welcomed the new initiative in the Congo townland. This was to be the flagship of the new scientific approach to coalmining in Tyrone. In 1891 a Manchester syndicate had acquired mining rights and an initial shaft had been sunk to a depth of 600 feet. Hopes ran high that it would prove one of the most remunerative coal tracts ever. Unfortunately, just when events were at their most promising, tragedy struck.

The intention of the Manchester syndicate was to postpone mining operations on an extensive scale until a communication had been opened up with an original Congo pit, now defunct. There had been numerous prospecting initiatives in the area but none of the pits had been worked to any great depth. As a consequence old workings were so prolific as to make work in the vicinity extremely dangerous. Advice had been sought from a government mining inspector, Mr William Saint from Manchester, who cautioned that until he arrived in person work should be curtailed. The company was aware of the dangers but at a later inquest it appeared that the inspector had reservations as to how his advice was followed. On the night of 10 December 1895 six lives were lost by drowning in the pit. Four were from Manchester and two were local. The men were on the night shift and had entered the pit at 11 p.m. Shortly before one o'clock the man employed at the bottom of the shaft to look after the 'hutches' or lorries experienced a strong gust of wind. His instincts told him that something was seriously amiss and he dashed for the ascent 'cage' which could accommodate four men. He was joined immediately by a fellow worker who had come from the shaft head. No sooner were they in the 'cage' than the water was upon them but they made it to the top and spread the alarm. The *Tyrone Courier* describes what happened next

> The silence of the night was broken by the sound of the whistle. This aroused the district and half-an-hour later the pit-mouth presented a heartrending spectacle … women and children pushed to the place, scantly clad, weeping and lamenting the death of their nearest and dearest.[35]

Four of the men were married, some with large families. One of the deceased, Fred Mitchell, was a weigh-clerk at the pit-head, and was only down the mine that night out of curiosity. Because of the water in the mine it was not possible to retrieve the bodies until four weeks later.[36] Of the eight men who went down the mine that night two came out alive. They were Thomas Ward and Edmund McMahon. At the time they both gave graphic accounts of what happened. McMahon's account is recalled here. It gives us a glimpse of the world of coalmining deep in the 'hill'. This was not a shallow mine; at any one time there might have been eleven to twenty-one people working below.[37]

Edmund McMahon described how

I went on duty at eleven o'clock, and went up the Congo 'jig'. On arrival at the top I found Edward Rafferty (the deputy), Cooper, and the two Bretlands. Cooper, William Bretland, and Rafferty were engaged at the face. David Bretland was filling a tub. I was ordered by Rafferty to go down the brow and bring up some timber. On the way down I met John McMullan (pump-man) and Fred Mitchell about half-way down the hill coming up together. I enquired from McMullan was there anything wrong. He replied that the pumps were getting too much water, and that he was going to get some of it stopped. McMullan asked me to go back with him again, but I replied I had been sent for timber, and that I had enough running up the brow without going back with him again.

So they continued up the hill, and I went down. When I reached the bottom of the jig I saw Ward, the 'bottomer', cleaning the water-course, and I enquired from him where the timber chain was. While looking for it at the foot of the 'jig' Ward said that there was a great wind. I replied that it was from the hutch, as it had begun to move up the brow. At that time a strong gust of wind came, which nearly knocked me down at the same time blowing the cap off Ward's head. It also extinguished the candles. I then said, 'make for the bell-wire, as there's something wrong'. We made our way there, and rang three knocks, got into the cage, and were wound up to the surface.[38]

The following day hundreds of people from Coalisland and Dungannon visited the scene. One of the first was the 'lord of the soil' the earl of Ranfurly, chairman of Dungannon Town Commissioners. The inquest into the tragedy on 31 January 1896 was not as conclusive as interested parties might have wanted or expected. In May 1896 a letter to the press sought a second inquest because the government inspector had raised questions regarding the findings of the original inquest which had exonerated the mining company of all blame.[39] There was a feeling locally that the air needed to be cleared on the matter. The managing director of the company, Donald Monro, had already sought a second inquest and had queried the evidence of the government inspector. Ranfurly and others were afraid that the official reservations on the government side as to what happened on the night did not bode well for the development of the area as a colliery district. However, from the government point of view the matter was now closed. Three years later the once-heralded Congo mining company experienced a nasty two-month strike by miners that involved charges of unlawful assembly, assault, and shots being fired before the matter was resolved at the end of January 1898. Mining continued at the pit until the end of the first decade of the twentieth century but 'only small quantities of coal continued to be raised'.[40] Later in the year another mining tragedy was to strike the community when there was an explosion in a newly opened mine at Annagher, owned by Corr and McNally.[41] Three men lost their lives, Bernard Murphy, Francis Girvan and John Hughes. The tragedy might have been worse if it had not been for the bravery of the under manager, Francis O'Neill, a native of Coalisland. He risked his life by going back down the mine to rescue others. A year later the Royal Humane Society (founded in 1744) awarded the Stanhope Gold Medal for gallantry to Francis O'Neill.[42] He was chosen out of 600 recommendations from all parts of the Empire and he was the second Irishman in 100 years to receive the award. The other Irishman was Major Torrens, retired officer of the Scots Grey, who lived in England. While the Congo and Annagher coal disasters marked the end of any major initiative in the Coalisland collieries until after the first world war, other industries, like spade making, established and maintained their own market niche.

Spade mills were widespread in northern Ireland in the nineteenth century. More than two-thirds of all spade mills in the country were in Ulster with an exceptional convergence of spade production in the Coalisland area.[43] Here, during the course of its operation no less than 240 different types of shovels and spade were manufactured.[44] Portlock in an attempt to show the 'beneficial applications of capital and power as are consequent on the proximity of coal' in 1843 gave an account of the 'extensive spade manufactory of Stewart Leckey Esq. established in Gortgonis townland (Coalisland) in the year 1834.' This industry employed 16 workers (two plaiters and four helpers, five finishers and five helpers) who worked through 40 weeks of the year. Portlock went on to say

> The workmen here are paid by the piece. Mr. Leckey allowing to the foremen 1s. 8d. per dozen for plaiting, and 4s. per dozen for finishing turf and common spades; and for shovels, 4s. 10d. per cwt. for plaiting and steeling, and 4s. for finishing. The foremen employ their own helpers, and pay them 6d. per dozen for plaiting, 1s. per dozen for finishing spades; 1s. 10d. per cwt. for plaiting and steeling, and 1s. per cwt for finishing shovels.
>
> This establishment is well conducted and appears to be in full employment. The water power has been hitherto found to be amply sufficient, and the possession of cheap fuel is an advantage, which ensures the successful prosecution of this branch of industry.[45]

Leckey's mill in the 1830s was a substantial operation and by the 1850s comprised two mills and five finishing houses. In 1858 John Stevenson bought the mills, together with saw and cornmills, a timber yard and stores. The site was on the Dungannon road out of Coalisland. Directly opposite in 1866 work began on the buildings that were to become the Coalisland Weaving Company when they opened their doors in 1868. The hammers in the spade mill were driven by three water wheels powered by a small mill-race known as 'the Green Bridge'.[46] There is no question but that the spade mill in Coalisland (fig. 8) was an important element in the town's developing

8 Coalisland Spade Mill.

economy. What may be less obvious was the centrality of the Coalisland mills to the spade industry in the north of Ireland itself. A close examination of, for instance, the Patterson family tree demonstrates this centrality. This locates members of the Patterson family over five generations working out of the Coalisland operation but significantly taking their skills to other places. The skills of plating, welding and finishing, involved in spade making were handed on from father to son. George Patterson worked the first known spade mill in Ballyroan in Co. Derry before 1780; and representatives of the next three generations worked at Coalisland. George Patterson's great grandson founded the mill at Templepatrick in Co. Antrim in the twentieth century. In 1980 it was considered to be the last spade mill maintaining 'a precarious existence'.[47] The Patterson family of Coalisland was there at the start of a unique tradition in spade making and was there at the end of an era.[48]

The final quarter of the nineteenth century was to see a remarkable transformation of Coalisland town as new names, traders and families came to prominence.[49] Some traditional industries such as coalmining went into terminal decline despite attempts to revive their fortunes, while linen factories continued to thrive. Old crafts expanded, especially spade making, and pottery and tile manufacture experienced more large-scale production. The transformation cannot be viewed in isolation, as extraordinary and far-reaching changes were already sweeping the larger economy of Great Britain. Coalisland had already established links with this outside economy in a special way from mid-century onwards. Now this link was to be further enhanced by

> The explosive rate of growth of Belfast during the period 1840–1880, a rather later emergence than in comparable English industrial cities, linked with the development of a wide range of manufactures and the creation of a great port in the flat, shallow estuary of the Lagan, [which] established that city as the focal point for the whole of the north, a development emphasised by the building of railways radiating from the city.[50]

By 1879 a branch of the Great Northern Railway was opened from Dungannon to Cookstown through Coalisland. Rail development presented a challenge to inland waterways. Ironically, in the 1890s traffic on the Coalisland canal increased more rapidly that at any previous period. Tonnage increased from 18,000 in 1890 to 36,000 in 1900.[51] This can be attributed to the privatisation of the canal, now in the ownership of the Lagan Navigation Company and away from the control of the Board of Works, where it was always seen as a loss-making venture. By 1901 Coalisland had certainly diversified its activities and now supported a larger population than hitherto but in terms of an industrial town it remained small. The 'take off' into real industrial growth failed to happen.

3. Coalisland in 1901

'The beginning of a little "Black Country" in Ireland'[1]

Between the 1830s and the 1880s the collective work experience of Coalisland is best summarised in terms of its coalmining activities, potteries and workshops and a developing textile industry. By the turn of the twentieth century there was a multitude of differentiated work experience. The 1901 Census for the town recorded over seventy different occupations and in excess of ninety distinct individual, more specialist, tasks. There were two reasons for this. First, the population had increased significantly, 29 per cent between 1881 and 1901. The greatest influx of people was into the south eastern side of the town. The town population of the Donaghenry parish end, in the west, dipped by 5 per cent in the same period. Between 1881 and 1901 the housing stock of the Donaghenry part of the town stayed more or less the same, suggesting a more settled part of the community. In contrast, the housing stock at the Tullyniskan parish end of the town doubled. Overall in the 20-year period the Coalisland housing stock increased by 32 per cent. Secondly, Coalisland was not immune to the 'massive transformation of the world economy'[2] that was taking place in the final quarter of the nineteenth century. Arguably, Coalisland with its developed system of communication via canal and railway was more open than other similarly sized settlements to the winds of economic change. Traditionally, economists have described the period 1873–96 as a time of 'Great Depression'. It was indeed a period of depression characterised by falling prices, falling profits, and greater competition. It was part of a worldwide phenomenon. Significantly, however, for the mass of people

> The quality of life improved for the majority of people as real wages went up and a wide variety of food and manufactured goods made their appearance in an increasing number of retail outlets, whilst industrial output continued to rise and trade continued to expand.[3]

Ireland shared in these developments and was

> in many respects a highly developed country by the end of the century. About half of its output – industrial and agricultural – was exported. Its major industries had an international renown, Belfast's liners, and linen, Irish whiskey and Dublin beer and biscuits having an unrivalled name. The country had an extensive banking and transport system. The

paradox to contemporaries was that, despite these circumstances, Ireland was not as prosperous as they would like to see it, and incomes compared to England and Scotland were relatively low.[4]

Megan McManus offers a good starting point for an examination of how this 'massive transformation' might have affected a small Ulster settlement.[5] McManus analyses *The Belfast and province of Ulster directories* published by the *Belfast News-Letter* in 1854, 1899, and 1916. By studying a number of sample settlements she attempted to explore the 'mentalities' behind small Ulster settlements and in particular what range of goods and services were available. Coalisland was not one of the sample. However, by examining the directories for 1854 and 1895 along with those that McManus used, we can set Coalisland in a wider context. The limitations of trade directories have been commented upon, particularly the levels of inconsistency, duplication, failure to record part-time or small-scale outlets.[6] To balance any such shortcomings an examination of the 1901 Census for Coalisland offers a fuller and more complete picture of the commercial growth of the town. This is particularly important for Coalisland where the level and range of commercial function and work experience appears to have been understated in the directories. In 1854 the maximum function range (number of goods and services) available in any sample settlement with a population between 500 and 1000 was 49. This was the town of Moneymore in Co. Derry. The minimum function range was 15; this was Rostrevor, in Co. Down. The mean function range was 27.4.[7] Coalisland with with a population of 627 had a function range of 15, equal to the minimum function range in McManus' study. Forty years later in 1895 Coalisland's population was 785 and according to the trade directory had a function range of 22. The range of goods and services available in the town appears not to have increased all that much. Yet in other settlements for 1899 the functions ranged from 17 to 69 with a mean of 38.3[8] If Coalisland were included in McManus' sample settlements it would have ranked third last in terms of function range, an obvious indicator of its failure to develop its potential. Yet Stewartstown, with a less obvious industrial past, three miles north of Coalisland had a population of 780 and a function range of 46 in 1899.[9] One explanation for this was the proximity of Coalisland to the market town of Dungannon and easy accessibility to a greater diversity of commercial function. This eased any economic need or gain in developing the commercial function range of Coalisland itself.

Coalisland in 1901 had a population of 875 comprising 180 families living in 177 houses, dominated by skilled artisans and semiskilled factory workers (65.6 per cent of the employed population). Twenty-three per cent were unskilled labourers and the remaining 11.6 per cent were shopkeepers, clerks, and a few other professionals viz. teachers, doctors, and one solicitor. Almost 60 per cent (57.7) of the workforce were under thirty years of age. Given the

presence of the Roan spinning mills and the weaving factory in the town
vicinity it might have been expected that the working population would
reflect the dominance of a female workforce. It was not the case. The labour
for these mills and factory appears to have been drawn from an area, west of
Coalisland town, and categorised in the 1901 census as the 'town of Brackaville'.
Ninety-six workers came from there with a further 65 coming from the rest of
the Brackaville townland. It was not uncommon for mill and weaving operatives
to travel up to six miles from surrounding townlands to work. A male labour
force dominated with a male-female ratio of 60–40. The dominant religion in
the town was Roman Catholic (77.6 per cent). The Church of Ireland con-
gregation was 16.5 per cent of the town population, followed by the
Presbyterian community (4.6 per cent, and others (0.9 per cent). There was
one Quaker and no Methodists nor Baptists.

By the turn of the century 72 per cent of the population of Coalisland
could read and write. Only 12 per cent were illiterate and 16 per cent could
read only. The importance of school attendance was central to literacy rates
and reflected the reading-book level reached on school exit. Literacy rates in
Coalisland for male and female were about the same (Table 2). Hepburn and
Collins[10] have shown that differential illiteracy between Catholics and Protestants
was a matter of some importance at the turn of the century. They found that
in Belfast twice as many Catholics were illiterate as Protestants. Comparable
figures for Coalisland show a 20 per cent lower literacy rate for the Catholic
population; and in proportionate terms *vis-à-vis* the Protestant community,
there were nearly four times as many Catholic illiterates.

Table 2. Literacy rates by sex and religion in Coalisland

Literacy	Males	%	Females	%	Catholics	%	Protestants	%
Cannot read/write	41	11.7	47	12.6	82	14.0	5	3.9
Read only	58	16.6	54	14.4	104	17.8	8	6.3
Read and write	249	71.5	272	72.9	397	68.0	114	89.8

Source: NA, 1901 census enumerators' schedule for Coalisland. Percentages based on
individuals five years old and upward

The high level of literacy at the end of the century prompts the perplexing
question whether this was in some way responsible or indeed a concomitant
factor in Coalisland's industrial character. Ever since C.A. Anderson con-
cluded, in an historical work on literacy in the developed world, that a 40 per
cent literacy rate can be regarded as a general threshold level for economic
development[11] the debate has raged whether literacy produces economic
growth or the other way round.[12] Anderson and Bowman both agreed that
the matter was far from clear-cut as 'literacy, like other elements in education,

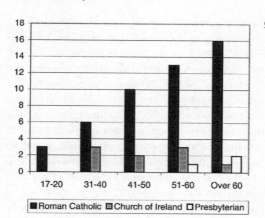

9 Numbers widowed in
   Coalisland by age, 1901

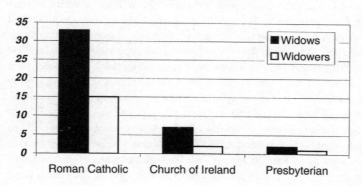

10 Total numbers widowed
    in Coalisland, 1901

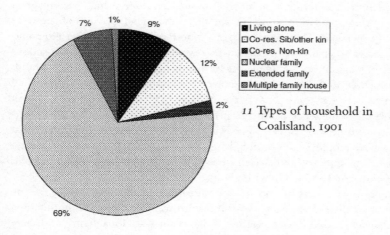

11 Types of household in
    Coalisland, 1901

is both a means of production and a consumer good, expenditure on which rises with income'.[13] Most recent research suggests that Anderson's figures exhibit no meaningful correlation in the 30 to 70 per cent literacy rate which was 'where most of the western economies found themselves during the period of industrial take-off'. Further, there is evidence to suggest 'that a literate workforce was of little relevance to the performance of the economy until it began to expand for exogenous reasons'.[14] Consequently, in the Coalisland context, literacy may have been a more important critical factor in economic growth in the 1830s and 1840s when exogenous growth was at an optimum, rather than later in the century when outside markets were well established. Significantly, the 1841 census records a literacy rate of 41 per cent for Coalisland town and sets it neatly in Anderson's schema.[15]

The average household in Coalisland was shaped by the perennial basic interaction of kinship, the family, wage economy and religion. Kinship was the most potent and primary source of living together. Most people were settled in households through marriage resulting in simple nuclear units with or without children. What is striking was the number of widows and widowers in the town (fig. 9 and fig. 10). There were sixty altogether with 40 per cent of them widowed before they were 50 years old. This may reflect not simply the death of a spouse but also an informal marital separation in a community, where the social pressure and the religious practice of the majority did not countenance divorce. Figure 11 shows a high proportion of families lived in simple nuclear units (69 per cent). Only 12 per cent of the population lived in households with other kin; only 9 per cent lived alone; and a mere 2 per cent lived with other unrelated men and women. On the night of the census there were 24 lodgers and 10 per cent of houses had the services of 24 domestic or general servants. The number of people living alone was small reflecting the absence of any state welfare for the sick and elderly. Miserly wages also worked against individuals trying to make ends meet living alone. A high percentage of the working population above the age of 17 and under 40 years of age were single (70 per cent). This is suggestive of a pattern of late marriage and also points to a greater acceptability of celibacy in a community where the endogamous nature of religion was absolute in the formation of households. Women as heads of household in Coalisland were returned as comprising 30.5 per cent of all householders. Of these 43.6 per cent were widows. Most did not work outside the home reflecting the deep-rooted family ideology of female dependence on a male wage earner.[16] The evidence from Coalisland demonstrates that unmarried employed sons and daughters remained at home supporting widowed parents and unmarried siblings. Two women heads of households were unmarried and living with a son and daughter each.

Interestingly, there are no street designations in the 1901 census for the town of Coalisland. A possible reason for this was that the streets in the town were partly located in two parishes, Tullyniskan and Donaghenry, and there was a requirement on the enumerator to make separate abstracts for each portion. By not returning the streets the town population was returned as a unity in their respective parishes. Despite this lack of naming we can form a good idea of what the town looked like. We do have a photograph of the main street around the turn of the century (fig. 12). Figure 13 gives a view of the Square in the town. The town has a prosperous appearance and this is also seen in the description of the quality of housing. Since the 1841 census housing in Ireland had been categorised in four classes. Coalisland in 1901 was credited with seven houses fulfilling the category of first class, 4 per cent of the housing stock. Most of the housing was rated second class (70 per cent). All of the first class housing had a minimum of eight rooms. The largest house in the town boasted 18 rooms and was occupied by a 23-year-old burly blacksmith from Fermanagh. Also in the house, on census night, was a 23-year-old servant girl from Donegal. Publicans, grocers, timber and grain merchants occupied these first class houses. One was occupied by a lady from the Cape of Good Hope in South Africa. She lived with her sister, two adopted children, a boarder and a servant.

In 1901 there were 180 families living in the town and 64 per cent of them were housed in two and three bedroomed houses. Only 17 per cent lived in accommodation of four rooms or more. Twelve of the houses had thatched roofs while the rest were made of slate or tile. In the photographs we have of Coalisland at this time it is noticeable how good the slating is on all houses, an indication of relative wealth in the community. The walls of the houses were made of stone or brick and the floors would have been tiled with tiles from the local potteries. For over 50 years local stone from the Carland quarries was well known and had a good reputation for building purposes. In the 1890s a limited company was formed by the Howard family in the area to bring renewed vigour to quarry excavation; shortly afterwards advertisements appeared in the local paper[17] offering work for up to 100 labourers paying 12s. a week. There was one family to each house with the exception two buildings. One of these was the Royal Ulster Constabulary barracks where the sergeant and one of his constables lived in five and two rooms respectively. By the end of the nineteenth century ideal standards of occupant density were considered to be no more than two persons to a room.[18] One to four persons, with a modal occupancy of two persons, lived in 60 per cent of the two-bedroomed houses. A further 29 per cent of two bedroomed houses accommodated five to seven occupants. Overcrowding was never an issue. Of the three-roomed homes 70 per cent fulfilled the ideal standard, with a modal occupation of five people. Well over half of all the houses in the town had only one or two windows to the front of the house. This limited natural light would have given the impression of darkness and dullness to the interiors. This innate drabness was not to be lightened.

In the town was a relatively small proportion of recent immigrants. Seventy-two of the adults in Coalisland originated outside of Tyrone. This

12 Main street Coalisland, *c.*1900.

represented almost 13 per cent of the workforce. Over half of these came from the counties of Armagh (12), Down (10), Antrim (9), Derry (7). Six originated in Scotland. Five came from Donegal and two of these were recorded by the census enumerators as the only two people in the town who spoke both Irish and English. Four originated in Fermanagh, three in Dublin, two in Leitrim and Monaghan, and one each in America, South Africa, Cork, Kildare, Kilkenny, Mayo, Wexford. Bernard Canning, a mechanical engineer, was the immigrant from Kildare. Jim Canning, his grandson, has been a potent force in the regeneration of the town in the final quarter of the twentieth century. Practically, all of these immigrants brought with them to the town a range of expertise whether it was in a trade such as carpentry or smithcraft, or services as in hostelry, bakery, medicine, law enforcement and railways. Business acumen was represented in the amount of drapers, dressmakers, grocers, and publicans who owed their origin to outside Tyrone.

Most of the people in Coalisland in 1901 were employed in factories. Coalisland ranked fourth as an industrial settlement in Tyrone at this time. Relative to its population it had a greater density of factories than either Dungannon or Cookstown and twice as many factories as Omagh in the west of the county. By 1901 the bulk of the Coalisland workforce was located in four major industries. The Ulster Fire Clay Works was set up in the townland of Derry in 1890. The proprietors Messrs Corr and McNally were ambitious to establish a pottery that would rival the famous ware of the 'Beleek' class.

THE SQUARE, COALISLAND, CO. TYRONE. 9044. W.L.

13 Coalisland Square, *c.*1900.

This particular initiative was not a success but the local paper praised 'the plucky attempt' and commended the owners for their other fireclay goods and coalmining initiatives that continued with 'unabated vigour'.[19]

The Tyrone Brick Company started up in 1898. Bricks had for years been made in the coal mining townlands of Gortnaskea and Derry for domestic needs but the Brick Company was the first to produce machine-made bricks.[20] The two main sources of work for Coalisland people besides the workshops mentioned were Roan's Spinning Mill in Brackaville (fig. 14) and the Weaving Factory (fig. 15) on the Dungannon road. The mill had some mill housing attached to it but nothing like the development seen in mill villages elsewhere.[21] The mill opened directly after the Famine in 1848 and was built up by the Wilson family who at the peak of production employed 250 people spinning flax into linen yarn.[22] Work began in the mill at 6.30 in the morning and finished at 6.30 in the evening. Wages in Roan Mills were ranked according to age and skill. The spinning and needle masters, and hacklers earned between 10*s*. and 12*s*. per week, the top wages for male workers. The wages for women were 8*s*. a week with young girls earning between 4*s*. and 8*s*. a week relative to age.[23] In the early years workers were paid in company tokens, which could only be spent in the Coalisland shops approved by the company. This was common practice in industrial villages elsewhere in Ulster. Shops became dependent on this custom and a strike in the mill, when it happened, had sharp repercussions on the commercial life of the town.

The Weaving Factory in Coalisland opened in 1868 and an examination of the workers' account book after 10 years in existence shows there were several differentiated job functions in the factory. Between weavers, doffers, men and boys, bundlers, reelers, machinists, and mechanics there were almost two hundred employed.[24] Working in the linen and weaving trade in the nineteenth century carried huge risks to personal health. Accidents in the Coalisland mill were rare enough and reported locally.[25] The most dangerous aspect was ' the omnipresence of dust in the preliminary processes and the great heat and moisture associated with spinning and, to a lesser extent, weaving. The latter was, on the whole, a healthier occupation than spinning and its ancillary processes.'[26] When the flax fibre first arrived at the mill it was subjected to hackling, a process that involved roughing, machine combing, and sorting. Huge volumes of dust were created in this process and workers were severely affected to the extent that respiratory ailments and 'bronchial irritation' were common complaints.[27] After hackling the raw product went to the preparatory rooms where an intricate order of operations – spreading, drawing and roving – made it ready for spinning. At this point a vast volume of 'pouce' or dust was released. This dust was much finer than that released in the hackling stage and was potentially more dangerous to the health of the worker. In this department the death rate from chest infections was very high.[28] In the weaving factory

> The weavers suffered greatly from chest infections caused by the stooping position necessary to the execution of their work and the damp hot atmosphere of the weaving shed. The death rate in this department was high, partly, because of the unhealthiness of the employment and partly because it was the practice for workers whose health had been undermined in the preparatory department to take up weaving.[29]

During the last quarter of the nineteenth century there were improvements in the equipment and structure of the mills and factories. The invention of the fan in 1873 brought relief in the reduction of dust particles, yet the use of fans in textile factories was ' quite exceptional'.[30] Both the Coalisland Weaving Factory and Roan Mills demonstrated an ability to move with the times. In the early 1890s Messrs L. Clarke and Sons, proprietors of the Factory, made extensive improvements in the workplace.[31] Roan Spinning Mill introduced machinery into the mill that reduced the number of hackling staff so fewer people were exposed to the dreaded 'pouce'.[32]

The nineteenth-century factory acts sought to improve the working conditions of the workers in the mills and textile factories but addressed the matter in piecemeal fashion. It was not until 1906 that far-reaching regulations concerning working conditions in the linen mills and factories were issued.[33] In the context of this study the 1871 Factory and Workshop Act was

14 Roan Spinning Mill, Coalisland, *c.*1901.

significant because it transferred the duty of enforcing the Workshop Acts from the local authorities to the Factory Inspectors. The effect of this for the linen trade was very good, at least in theory. It made for greater visitation and attention to individual workplaces. In practice, it led to wholesale complaints from the sub-inspectors who had to carry out the visitations. Dawkins Cramp, sub-inspector of the north Irish sub-division declared:

> in one year I have only been able to visit one-third of the workshops in addition to my ordinary factory work, and this has been done at very great inconvenience, and after all, not very satisfactorily, and I do not see how I can in the future do more than I have in the past. So that it would take three years to visit all the workshops even once, and they might as well not be visited at all.[34]

Cramp calculated that in his district of Antrim, Londonderry, Tyrone, Donegal and part of Down there were 485 factories, about 1,750 workshops, and 3,405 scutching mills. Eight factories and ten workshops were located in Coalisland. He went on to report that the workshop acts were only partially enforced in the north of Ireland and that two-thirds of the workshops were run in entire ignorance of what was required according to law.

Whenever the Wilson family, owners of Roan Mills, launched a new lighter in the canal basin several hundred spectators would arrive for the

MILLS AND RAILWAY STATION COALISLAND.DUNGANNON,CO.TYRONE.9047.W.L.

15 Coalisland Weaving Factory and rail station, c.1900.

launch. It was a mark of how well the mills were doing that the tonnage capacity for a new lighter (75 tons) was half that again of the average lighter that plied between Coalisland and Belfast.[35] The death in 1891 of Mrs. Jennie Wilson (at 43 years of age), wife of Henry Wilson, the mill proprietor, was a setback for the mill employees. She had taken a great interest in the young women in her husband's employment and 'did everything to enlighten and improve them as well as cheer them in their work and duties'.[36] In the years that followed industrial relations in the mill took a turn for the worst. The last quarter of the nineteenth century was a very disappointing time for the linen industry as the volume of piece goods and yarn declined. Not alone was demand slack everywhere but prices contracted.[37] Trade picked up in the final decade of the century and workers attempted to recoup some of the losses sustained in poor times. In 1893 there was a strike in the Dungannon mills when the boys who attended the machines wanted 2s. more per week. They did not succeed and had to return to work without it. During early 1894 the weaving and linen workers in Coalisland were on reduced hours and just when this had been sorted out, the management in the Coalisland mills reduced wages by 1d. a day.[38] The female workers refused to return to work. The mill was closed and the 'greatest depression' descended on the local shops in consequence.[39] The mill did re-open but its later history suggests lessons were not learned. In 1915 the mill closed for a year when Henry Wilson refused to countenance a wage increase. He relented and grudgingly agreed the pay increase. The mill re-opened only to find that key workers had disappeared and the market had been lost to cheaper Russian goods. It closed again and reopened under Sir Samuel Kelly after the war. It shut down finally in 1926 with the loss of 200 jobs and the chimney and mill row were demolished.[40] The weaving factory closed in 1980.

If the physical and economic worlds of Coalisland are relatively straight-forward to reconstruct the mental world of the inhabitants is elusive. In the early part of the nineteenth century Archbishop Curtis thought that the laity believed and practiced nothing more than heathen superstition.[41] There was, indeed, a limited religious practice in attendance at chapel and a limited range of devotional observances before the Famine.[42] Tyrone in the nineteenth century was one of the poorer counties. Coalisland, at the northern end of the Armagh diocese, was geographically remote for generations from the centre of administration, which was Drogheda.[43] Being poor and remote meant slow progress in church building. An Ordnance Survey Memoir noted that the chapel in Stewartstown, three miles from Coalisland, was built in 1797 and repaired in 1807. It had no seats but could hold 450 people.[44] This first chapel, a small thatched building, gave rise to a lawsuit which ended up in the Dublin courts with Daniel O'Connell.[45] Between 1843 and 1849 Peter Daly built a chapel in Stewartstown. For the first half of the century the Stewartstown building was the parish chapel of the Coalisland Catholics. It was not until the late 1850s that a chapel was built in Brackaville, just outside Coalisland by the Revd James Daly. He died in an accident shortly afterwards in 1861 in America where he had gone to raise funds for the new cathedral in Armagh.

A virtual renaissance in Roman Catholic thought and practice took place in Ireland during the course of the nineteenth century as a new sense of religious identity began to take shape. The term 'devotional revolution' was used in 1972 by the American historian Emmet Larkin to explain what he saw as a 'sudden and dramatic transformation of popular religious practice in Ireland in the period *c.*1850–1875'.[46] There are clues that the 'devotional revolution' in Coalisland was slow to catch on. When Paul Cullen, fresh from Rome, was appointed archbishop of Armagh in 1849 he was reportedly appalled by the state of religion in the diocese and set about initiating new devotional practices.[47] When he was appointed archbishop of Dublin Armagh priests dropped many elements in his 'devotional revolution'. Joseph Dixon, a Coalisland man and former Maynooth professor succeeded Cullen as archbishop in Armagh. Dixon found himself on more than one occasion having to deal with clerical tardiness. One of the cornerstones in the new religious fervour was the parish mission. In the Dixon papers an episode detailed how the parish priest of Coalisland locked visiting missionary priests out of their house because of new devotional practices they appeared to be promulgating. The missioners were forced to flee to Dungannon for shelter.[48]

We do not know the level of Catholic religious practice in Coalisland at the close of the century. We do know, from the detail of vestry minutes, that there was concern in the Church of Ireland parish of Tullyniskan about a drastic decline in church attendance during the 1890s. A section of the community in Coalisland was part of this parish. Attendances averaged 123 at morning service and 39 at evening service, with those taking communion dropping to an average of 16.[49] In 1891 there were 200 Church of Ireland families with a total church population of 731. In 1905 there were only 125 families, a drop of 37.5 per cent. The reasons for this are not clear, as the minister, Mr Lindsay, was both 'very dutiful and industrious'.[50]

One common social problem besetting both chapel and church in the nineteenth century was the demon drink. Both Catholic and Protestant authorities approached the matter rather differently. Catholic authorities distanced themselves from movements of total abstinence.[51] They did so partly because Protestants were in the vanguard of such movements and partly they recognized how deeply ingrained social habits of the Irish were and that to advocate a radical change in social habits could undermine their authority.[52] It could also be argued that there was a definite question of clerical ambivalence on the matter:

> ... fondness for drink remained an abiding curse among some. There were complaints from various parishes of priests being too drunk to say Mass, and in one instance in March 1866 a report of a clergyman who had died 'from drink'. More typical, perhaps, was the case of the Rev. Mr. Quinn, the parish priest of Donaghmore,[53] who after repeated warnings was suspended for having broken his pledge, and Peter Daly of Coalisland who suffered a similar fate for his lack of discipline.[54]

Cochrane's corner in Coalisland was often the cockpit for pugilistic encounters on a Sunday evening, when drink was taken. Disgraceful scenes reportedly happened there and the town's policemen were constantly on the alert.[55] In February 1891 Constable Grainey was transferred to Dungannon and there was much local regret at his going because he was credited with 'cleaning up the drink scene' during his sojourn in the town.[56] In 1891 Mrs Patterson sought to renew her mother's public house licence. The police advised the court of petty sessions at Stewartstown that there were too many pubs in the neighbourhood. The pub in question was half-a-mile from the town and too far from police supervision.[57] The community made valiant efforts to get on top of the problem. The town had its own Teetotal Society and summer outings recall times of simple pleasures and a world long since gone. The Society's train excursion to the seaside resort of Warrenpoint was often

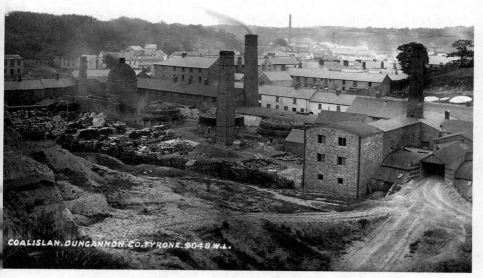

COALISLAN.DUNGANNON.CO.TYRONE.9048.W.L.

16 Coalisland town from Annagher Hill, *c.*1900.

anticipated with great eagerness. Dressmakers were in big demand in the week beforehand, some working into the Sunday morning of the excursion in order to meet the demand for finery. Millinery establishments in the town 'were ransacked' and on the morning of the excursion the Teetotal Brass Band paraded and played their way from the Church to the railway station. When the train returned at 9.15 in the evening it was met by cheering crowds.[58] Feastdays were always a headache for the local constabulary and gave good copy to those who thought that Coalisland had a reputation for 'its sheebeens, houses of ill-fame, and other classic establishments in more than the usual variety and number'.[59]

Sectarian and political tension between Protestant and Catholic communities was rare enough in Coalisland at the turn of the century. Occasionally, there was the odd rumpus and riot. On one occasion in 1892 Orangemen returning home from Portrush from an excursion were met by 500 nationalists at Dudgeon's corner in the town. A fracas ensued; stones were fired and up to 60 people were brought to court.[60] St Patrick's day in the town was a potential powder keg and it was often necessary to bring in an extra force of up to 30 policemen. Their function was to walk the streets and act as a deterrent to any potential malcontents. It worked, though certainly on one occasion their presence reportedly turned the festival into ' a dull day in Coalisland '.[61] Cross community support was clearly seen in the setting up of the Congo disaster fund when the churches came together to raise money for the families of the miners who had perished in the coal-mine in 1895. The response from all sides of the community was magnificent.[62] The target for the fund was £1,000 and within a month £600 had been collected and lodged to the bank.[63]

In addition to religion there were other ways of passing the time in Coalisland. Temperance cafes and 'self-improving' public meetings in modern community halls were encouraged. The widely accepted educative principle of 'a sound mind in a sound body' saw a crusade to embrace all forms of outdoor pursuits like cycling, swimming, football playing and spectating. Yet, despite all these new leisure ways it appeared that 'the public house was central to the social life of the population'.[64] Coalisland was no different. In its own way it mirrored the activities that were central to a more urban population. A local coffee house was established in 1885. An amateur concert was held in the Protestant hall in the town to raise funds for its maintenance. In order that the hall would be more user-friendly and help cultivate other pursuits local merchant, John Stevenson, wainscotted, painted, seated, lighted, and improved the hall at his own expense.[65] In the 1890s the Catholic community saw the need to erect an extra storey on St Patrick's hall in order to facilitate a reading room and accommodate a billiard table. A drama club was set up in 1894.[66] Touring drama groups like the Warwick Buckland Company were no strangers to the area.[67] The Mexican circus, when it visited, was a huge draw not least because Johnny Patterson, the famous Irish clown, was travelling with it.[68] In towns generally public libraries expanded. Reading pursuits were encouraged through the good auspices of the *Tyrone Courier* newspaper. It had a circulating library and often had surplus novels for sale.[69] These included the works of renowned authors such as George Meredith, Walter Scott, R.L. Stevenson, Anthony Trollope, Mark Twain, Charlotte Younge and others. Music, particularly band music, was very popular. There were bands everywhere: the Coalisland Brass band, the Coalisland Flute band, the Creenagh Flute band, the Dirnagh Flute Band, Ballinderry Brass and Mahon Flute bands. The bands received first class tuition from local and amateur musicians.[70] Fishing in the historic Roughan Lough, in the townland of Roughan, was a favourite past time for some. On occasion it could yield up a record-breaking pike weighing 17lbs.[71] It was the train, the excursion train, that introduced most workers to a world beyond their own. The Great Northern Railway arrived in Coalisland in 1879 and was quick to see the advantages of mass travel for the proletariat. Small fashionable resorts, like Portrush and Warrenpoint were opened up to the masses. Day excursions to Portrush were very popular for the employees of Roan Spinning mill and the Weaving Factory. When both companies went on a joint excursion up to seven hundred people travelled.[72] The Cookstown horse races were a major draw for the Coalisland people. Invariably, local horses ran well there. Interestingly, those people who travelled but had no interest in the races found that they could regale themselves with some fine cock-fighting nearby.[73] For those Coalisland people who aspired to other recreational pursuits there was, in nearby Dungannon, a dynamic cycling club as well as an enterprising lawn tennis club.

In the period 1800 to 1901 Coalisland town experienced the most momentous and far-reaching changes in its chequered history. In the early 1800s when the Coalisland region boasted resources in coal and clay, that made it unique in Ireland, Coalisland town was a mere settlement. By 1901 the town population had quadrupled in the course of the century, housing density increased, and the town of Coalisland now 'dominated' the region. All the appearances of a little 'Black Country' were beginning to emerge (fig. 16). The 1901 census profiles a town predominantly Catholic with a high rate of literacy and less than 25 per cent of the labour force classed as unskilled. The town had a thriving linen mill, a weaving factory, the Ulster Fireclay works, the Tyrone Brick Company, numerous workshops, and a range of shops and public houses. The population was well off, relative to the surrounding town-lands. People from elsewhere found it worthwhile to gravitate to and settle down in the town. It had a youthful population. Six out of 10 of the work-force were under 30 and seven out of 10 people between the ages of 17 and 40 were not married. Folk memory suggests that by the end of the century there were up to 1000 people employed in the town and its environs. Coalisland, with a developed system of communications via canal and railway (since 1879), was well poised to take advantage of the transformation in world economic markets in the final quarter of the century. In the 1890s traffic on the canal increased more rapidly than at any previous period.[74] In 1901 Coalisland's success as an industrial settlement was beyond doubt.

Conclusion

Traditionally, the term Industrial Revolution was understood to mean a sudden break with the past and was used to describe the period of massive industrial change from 1750 onwards. The salient characteristics of the phenomenon were large-scale production, the use of steam power and machinery, employment of large numbers in factories and market expansion. Population growth and urbanisation were further manifestations.

Understood in this way, Ireland never experienced the Industrial Revolution in the nineteenth century. Today, however, 'the idea of a sudden break has been replaced by an emphasis on gradual incremental change that differed in its pace and nature from one region to another'.[1] Among historians, the emphasis has moved to focus on the notion of continuity with earlier industrial developments. There is a growing realization that 'the term Industrial Revolution does not have a precise meaning but can only be used as a convenient general description'.[2] In this new paradigm the present study of the industrial growth of Coalisland, in east Tyrone, in the nineteenth century is important.

In our new understanding of what the Industrial Revolution was about historians need to look at 'little developments' that reflect continuity and change. This study posits Coalisland as a model of a 'little development' between 1800 and 1901, a microcosm of the Industrial Revolution elsewhere. All the ingredients were there. Coal was present to be mined in abundance. There was a move towards large-scale production from cottage industry to the arrival of steam power in the establishment of a spinning mill (1848) and a weaving factory (1868). Large numbers were employed under one roof. Workshops thrived and markets expanded. During the period the population of the town quadrupled and the Coalisland community adapted to meet the challenge of social and economic change.

The world economy experienced a massive transformation, in the coming of the mass market, in the final quarter of the nineteenth century and this had an impact on Coalisland. The transformation, to an extent, cloaked the very real difficulties in the Coalisland economy of inadequate resourcing and unsatisfactory husbandry of what resources that were there. Local entrepreneurs attempted in the 1870s to renew their efforts to make the collieries commercially viable. They failed.

Questions remain. Given Coalisland's head start as an industrial settlement in the 1830s and 1840s could more have been expected, when the markets were transformed everywhere at the end of the century? Was there a failure of nerve? Given the predominance of the Roman Catholic ethos in the town at the turn of the century, what correlation, if any, may be made with the absence of a Protestant ethic and industrial progress? In comparison with other comparable settlements, which had little industrial tradition, why was the function range of goods and services in Coalisland so limited? Was there a break, a closing down of entrepreneurial spirit as older family names, prominent between 1830 and the late 1870s, disappeared? In 1901 the business acumen of Coalisland rested with 'outsiders' who were to the fore in the commercial life of the town. Coalmining, once the town's *raison dêtre*, had all but disappeared at the end of the century. What else may have died with it and what legacy was carried forward into the twentieth century and beyond?

The vital question must be what happens to a community in which great expectations fell well short of reality in three successive centuries. In the early eighteenth century there was growing optimism among learned opinion in Dublin that Tyrone coal was better, found in greater quantities and could be more reliably sourced than the annual import of coal into Ireland from English and Scottish ports.[3] It was 'confidently calculated' that Dublin, the second city of the Empire, could be supplied with coal from the Coalisland area for 'a period of at least half a century'.[4] It didn't happen. In the nineteenth century, in this study, we have seen expectations raised again and fizzle out. In the early twentieth century we know of Sir Samuel Kelly's heroic efforts to mine coal when over two hundred miners were brought in from outside. The initiative ended abruptly and in failure. What remains is a rugged independence, glimpsed in Hardman's account of the *mentalité* of the miners in the early 1870s. It has not gone away. Tradition dies hard – the nineteenth-century weaving factory, now closed, today plays host to any number of entrepreneurs who rent workshops there. Yet again, Coalisland re-invents itself and the rest is history.

Notes

ABBREVIATIONS

AAA   Archives of the Archdiocese of Armagh, Ó Fiaich Library, Armagh.
CI   Church of Ireland
HC   House of Commons
LGD   Local Government District
NA   National Archives
NI   Northern Ireland
OS   Ordnance Survey
PRONI Public Record of Northern Ireland
RC   Roman Catholic
RDS   Royal Dublin Society

INTRODUCTION

1 M. Dillon, 'Coalisland: the evolution of an industrial landscape' in *Studia Hibernica*, no. 8, (1968), p. 81.
2 Ibid., p. 81.
3 A. Day and P. McWilliams (eds), *Ordnance survey memoirs of Ireland*, xx (Belfast, 1993), p. 141.
4 *Poor Inquiry*, HC., 1836, xxxii, appendix E.
5 Ibid., p. 37.
6 P.R.O.N.I., Val/1b/66a.
7 W.R. Hutchison, *Tyrone precinct* (Dundalk, 1951).
8 W.A. McCutcheon, *The industrial archaeology of Northern Ireland* (Belfast, 1980). This gives a splendid overview of the history of the collieries over the course of three centuries.
9 R. Griffith, *Geological and mining surveys of the coal districts of the counties of Tyrone and Antrim* (Dublin, 1829).
10 J.E. Portlock, *Geological report on Londonderry and parts of Tyrone and Fermanagh* (Dublin, 1843).
11 E.T. Hardman, 'On the present state of coalmining in the county of Tyrone' in

the *Journal of the Royal Dublin Society*, vi (1875), pp 366–83.
12 M.McManus, 'The potteries of Coalisland, county Tyrone: some preliminary notes' in *Ulster Folklife*, 30, (1984), p. 67.
13 Dillon, 'Coalisland: the evolution of an industrial landscape', p. 95.
14 W.R. Hutchison, *Tyrone precinct* (Dundalk, 1951), p. 135.
15 Ibid., p. 140.
16 D.S. Macneice, 'Factory workers' housing in counties Down and Armagh', unpublished PhD thesis, Queen's University Belfast, 1981.
17 D.S. Macneice, 'Industrial villages of Ulster, 1800–1900' in P. Roebuck (ed.), *Plantation to partition*, (Belfast, 1981), pp 172–190.
18 Ibid., p.182.

I. COALISLAND BEFORE THE FAMINE

1 S. Lewis, *A topographical dictionary of Ireland* (3 vols., London, 1837), i, p. 383.

2 Dillon, 'Coalisland: the evolution of an industrial landscape', p. 94.

3 J. McEvoy, *A statistical survey of county Tyrone 1802* (reprint, Belfast, 1991), p. 21.

4 W.R. Hutchison, *Tyrone precinct* (Dundalk, 1951), p. 142.

5 PRONI, Val/1D/6/4.

6 PRONI, Val/1b/66a.

7 Lewis, *A topographical dictionary of Ireland*, i, p. 384.

8 A. Day and P. McWilliams (eds), *Ordnance survey memoirs of Ireland*, xx (Belfast, 1993), p. 43.

9 Lewis, *A topographical dictionary of Ireland*, i, p. 384.

10 Ibid.

11 Ibid.

12 *Poor Inquiry*, H.C., 1836, xxxi., appendix D.

13 J.E. Portlock, *Geological report on Londonderry and parts of Tyrone and Fermanagh* (Dublin, 1843), p. 603.

14 Ibid., p. 604.

15 Ibid., p. 602.

16 Ibid., p. 606.

17 Ibid.

18 Ibid.

19 Ibid., p. 607.

20 Ibid., p. 608.

21 Day and McWilliams (eds), *Ordnance survey memoirs of Ireland*, xx, p. 29.

22 Ibid., p. 43

23 J.E. Portlock, *Geological report on Londonderry and parts of Tyrone and Fermanagh* (Dublin, 1843), p. 620.

24 Ibid., p. 622.

25 Ibid., p. 623.

26 Ibid., p. 626.

27 McCutcheon, *The industrial archaeology of Northern Ireland* (Belfast, 1980), p. 337.

28 E.T. Hardman, ' On the present state of coalmining in the county of Tyrone 'in the *Journal of the Royal Dublin Society*, vi (1875), p. 366.

29 Ibid., p. 378.

30 McCutcheon, *The industrial archaeology*, p. 339.

31 McEvoy, *A statistical survey*, p. 25–26.

32 McManus, 'The potteries of county Tyrone, in *Ulster Folklife* 30 (1984), p. 68.

33 Day and McWilliams (eds), *Ordnance survey memoirs of Ireland*, xx, p. 30.

34 Ibid., p. 29–30.

35 Ibid., p. 139.

36 Ibid., p. 140.

37 Ibid.

38 Portlock, *Geological report*, p. 680.

39 Ibid., p. 681.

40 Ibid.

41 *Census of Ireland 1831, with comparative abstract, as taken in 1821*, HC, 1833 (23) xxxix, 3.

42 J. J. Lee, 'On the accuracy of the pre-famine Irish censuses' in J.M. Goldstrom and L.A. Clarkson (eds), *Irish population, economy and society: essays in honour of the late K.H. Connell* (Oxford, 1981), p. 41.

43 *Census of Ireland 1831*, HC., 1833 (634) xxxix, 59.

44 McCutcheon, *The industrial archaeology*, p. 335.

45 Quoted in McCutcheon, *The industrial archaeology*, p. 335.

46 F. Mendels, ' Proto-industrialisation: The first phase of the industrialisation process ', in *Journal of Economic History*, 32 (1972), pp 241–61.

47 R. Houston and K. Snell, 'Proto-industrialisation? Cottage industry, social change, and industrial revolution', in *Historical Journal*, 27, 2, (1984), pp 473–92.

2. COALISLAND AFTER THE FAMINE

1 E.T. Hardman, 'On the present state of coal mining on the county of Tyrone' in the *Journal of the Royal Dublin Society*, 6, (1875). p. 373.

2 Hardman, p. 373.

3 R. Marsh, *A history of Brackaville parish* (Dungannon, 1981), p. 9.

4 *Parliamentary select committee report on industry*, HC, 1885, (288) ix 1. pp 472–3.

5 McManus, ' The potteries of county Tyrone', p. 7.

6 M. Dillon, 'Coalisland: the evolution of an industrial landscape', in *Studia Hibernica*, 8, (1968), p. 88.

7 F.W. Smith, *Irish linen trade handbook and directory*, p. 128.

8 Ibid., p. 135.

9 *Census of Ireland*, 1871, Vol. III, H.C., 1874, lxxiv, pt I, 1.

10 *Census of Ireland*, 1881,Vol. III [c.3204], H.C., 1882, lxxviii, 1.

11 *Census of Ireland*, 1891,Vol. 1112 [c.6626], H.C., 1892, xcii, 1.

12 Hardman, 'On present state of coalmining', p. 369.

13 Ibid., p. 371.

14 Ibid., p. 373.

15 Ibid., p. 374.

16 Ibid., p. 372.

17 *Tyrone Courier,* 14 Jan 1893.

18 Hardman, 'On the present state of coalmining', p. 375.

19 Ibid., p.379.

20 Ibid., p.376.

21 PRONI, D/1905/1/12.

22 PRONI, D/1905/1/12, D/1905/1/14, D/1905/1/15 Liquidation papers of the Tyrone Coal Mining Company.

23 The new company was officially registered on 9 April 1877 with the Registrar's Office in England.

24 This appointment was to lead to High Court proceedings in 1886 when Evans declared that he had not been paid for his services as secretary.

25 PRONI, D/1905/1/12. Letter from liquidator to shareholders, 16 June 1879.

26 PRONI, D/1905/1/12.

27 *Tyrone Courier,* 4 July 1891.

28 Hardman, 'On the present state of colamining', p. 377.

29 *Tyrone Courier,* 12 Nov 1892.

30 Ibid., 10 June 1893.

31 Hardman, 'On the present state of coalmining'.

32 *Tyrone Courier,* 31 March 1894.

33 Ibid., 7 July 1894.

34 *Belfast Newsletter,* 16 March 1895.

35 *Tyrone Courier,* 14 Dec 1895.

36 Ibid., 25 Jan 1896.

37 Ibid., 8 Feb 1896.

38 Ibid., 14 Dec 1895.

39 Ibid., 30 May 1896.

40 W.R. Hutchinson, *Tyrone precinct* (Dundalk, 1951), p. 147.

41 *Tyrone Courier,* 6 Oct 1889.

42 *Mid-Ulster Mail,* 5 Aug 1899.

43 The Coalisland spade mill is now reconstructed in Cultra Folk Museum, Belfast.

44 *Tyrone Courier and News,* Millennium Souvenir Special, 29 Dec. 1999.

45 J.E. Portlock, *Geological report on Londonderry and parts of Tyrone and Fermanagh,* (Dublin 1843), p. 685.

46 R. Marsh, *A history of Brackaville parish* (Dungannon, 1981), p. 9.

47 W.A. McCutcheon, *The industrial archaeology of Northern Ireland* (1980), p. 260.

48 'Coalisland spade factory', museum pamphlet, Cultra, Co. Down.

49 See the *Belfast and Provincial Towns' Directory,* 1852–1900.

50 W.A. McCutcheon, *The canals of the north of Ireland* (London, 1965), p.79.

51 Ibid., p. 81.

3. COALISLAND IN 1901

1   W.A. McCutcheon, *The canals of the north of Ireland,* (London, 1965), p. 80.

2   H.W.Fraser, *The coming of the mass market, 1850–1914* (London, 1981), p. x.

3   B.J. Smales, *Economic history* (London, 1981), p. 141.

4   L.M. Cullen, *An economic history of Ireland since 1660* (London, 1987), p. 167.

5   M. McManus, 'The functions of small Ulster settlements in 1854, 1899 and 1916', in *Ulster Folklife,* 39, (1993), pp 50–72.

6   Ibid., p. 51.

7   Ibid., p. 52.

8   Ibid., p. 58.

9   Ibid., p. 58.

10 A. C. Hepburn and B. Collins, 'Industrial society: the structure of Belfast, 1901', in P. Roebuck (ed.), *Plantation to partition* (Belfast, 1981), pp 218–19.

11 C.A. Anderson, 'Literacy and schooling on the development threshold, some historical cases' in C.A. Anderson and M.J. Bowman (eds), *Education and economic development* (London, 1965).

12 E.G. West, 'Literacy and the industrial revolution' in *Economic History Review,* 2nd series, 31, no. 3, (1978), p. 369.

13 M.J. Bowman and C.A. Anderson, 'Concerning the role of education in development' in C. Geertz (ed.), *Old societies and new states* (New York, 1963), p. 250.

14 D.Vincent, *The rise of mass literacy* (Cambridge, 2000), p. 83.

15 *Census of Ireland 1841,* [504], H.C., 1843, xxiv, 1.

16 M. Cohen, *Linen, family and community in Tullylish, County Down, 1690–1914* (Dublin, 1997), p. 203.
17 *Tyrone Courier*, 21 May 1892.
18 Macneice, 'Industrial villages of Ulster, 1800–1900', p. 188.
19 *Tyrone Courier*, 16 May 1891.
20 Ibid., 29 Dec 1899.
21 T. Hunt, *Portlaw, County Waterford, 1825–1876* (Dublin, 2000), p. 11.
22 *Tyrone Courier*, 29 Dec 1899.
23 Ibid.
24 Workers' account book, fortnight ending 16 February 1878, located in Coalisland Heritage Centre, Coalisland.
25 *Tyrone Courier*, 16 June 1894.
26 D.C. Armstrong, 'Social and economic conditions in the Belfast linen industry' *Irish Historical Studies* (1951), p. 245.
27 Ibid., p. 246.
28 Ibid., p. 248.
29 Ibid., p. 250.
30 Ibid., p. 252.
31 *Tyrone Courier*, 12 Nov. 1891.
32 Ibid.
33 Armstrong, 'Social and economic conditions in the Belfast linen industry', p. 252.
34 *Reports of inspectors of factories, May-October 1872*, HC, 1873 [c.745] xix, 41. p. 127.
35 *Tyrone Courier*, 1 Oct 1892.
36 Ibid., 28 Feb 1891.
37 Armstrong, 'Social and economic conditions in the Belfast linen industry', p. 239.
38 *Tyrone Courier*, 31 March 1894.
39 Ibid., 7 July 1894.
40 Ibid., *Tyrone Courier* (Millennium supplement), 29 Dec 1999.
41 AAA., Curtis Papers, Folder no. 2.
42 E. Larkin, *The historical dimensions of Irish Catholicism* (Dublin, 1976), p. 7.
43 A. Macaulay, 'Catholicism in nineteenth-century Tyrone' in C. Dillon, and H. A. Jefferies (eds), Tyrone: *history and society* (Dublin, 2000), p. 617.
44 Day, and McWilliams (eds), *Ordnance survey memoirs of Ireland*, xx, p. 38.
45 McGarvey, Rev. C. 'A history of Coalisland [Church]', in *Tyrone Democrat Supplement*, May, 1980. Aidan Fee disputes O'Connell's involvement

finding no evidence to support the claim in *The Bell* (Journal of Stewartstown and District local history society) 5 (1993), pp 66–72.
46 S.J. Connolly (ed.), *The Oxford companion to Irish history* (Oxford, 1998), p. 145.
47 O.P. Rafferty, *Catholicism in Ulster, 1603–1983* (Dublin 1994), p. 135.
48 AAA., Dixon papers, Folder no. 7.
49 E. Donnelly, *Commitment being our challenge, a history of the parish of Tullynisken, Newmills, County Tyrone* (Dungannon, 1993), p. 72.
50 Ibid.
51 Connolly, *Religion and society in nineteenth century Ireland*, p. 55.
52 Ibid.
53 Donaghmore was three miles from Coalisland.
54 Rafferty, *Catholicism in Ulster*, p. 152.
55 *Tyrone Courier*, 31 Jan, 4 July 1891.
56 Ibid., 28 Feb 1891.
57 Ibid., 16 May 1891.
58 Ibid., 4 July 1891.
59 Ibid., 15 Aug 1891.
60 Ibid., 13 Aug 1892.
61 Ibid., 23 March 1893.
62 Ibid., 21 Dec 1895.
63 Ibid., 11 Jan 1896.
64 Fraser, *The coming of the mass market*, p. 208.
65 *Tyrone Courier*, 6 Feb 1885.
66 Ibid., 4 Feb 1894.
67 Ibid., 1 Sept 1894.
68 Ibid., 16 Oct 1885.
69 Ibid., 12 August 1893.
70 Ibid., 4 Nov 1893.
71 Ibid., 16 June 1894.
72 Ibid., 7 Sept 1899.
73 Ibid., 16 May 1891.
74 McCutcheon, *The canals of the north of Ireland* (London, 1965), p. 79.

CONCLUSION

1 D. Hey (ed.), *The Oxford companion to local and family history* (Oxford, 1998), p. 231.
2 Ibid.
3 Hutchison, *Tyrone precinct*, p. 133.
4 Day and Williams (eds), *Ordnance Survey memoirs of Ireland*, xx, p. 30.